THE POWER OF REGRET

Also by Daniel H. Pink

Free Agent Nation

A Whole New Mind

The Adventures of Johnny Bunko

Drive

To Sell Is Human

When

THE
POWER
OF REGRET

*How Looking Backward
Moves Us Forward*

//

Daniel H. Pink

RIVERHEAD BOOKS

NEW YORK

2022

RIVERHEAD BOOKS
An imprint of Penguin Random House LLC
penguinrandomhouse.com

Grateful acknowledgment is made for permission to reprint the following:
page 61, tweet copyright © 2020 by Ely Kreimendahl. Used with permission.

Library of Congress Cataloging-in-Publication Data

Names: Pink, Daniel H., author.
Title: The power of regret: how looking backward moves us forward / Daniel
H. Pink. Description: New York: Riverhead Books,
2022. | Includes bibliographical
references and index. Identifiers: LCCN 2021036660 (print) |
LCCN 2021036661 (ebook) |
ISBN 9780735210653 (hardcover) | ISBN 9780735210677 (ebook)
Subjects: LCSH: Regret. Classification: LCC BF575.R33 P56 2022 (print) |
LCC BF575.R33 (ebook) |
DDC 152.4—dc23

LC record available at https://lccn.loc.gov/2021036660
LC ebook record available at https://lccn.loc.gov/2021036661

International edition ISBN: 9780593541487

Printed in the United States of America
1st Printing

Book design by Amanda Dewey

CONTENTS

"Though we would like to live without regrets, and sometimes proudly insist that we have none, this is not really possible, if only because we are mortal."

James Baldwin, 1967

THE POWER OF REGRET

Part One

REGRET RECLAIMED

//

1.

The Life-Thwarting Nonsense
of No Regrets

On October 24, 1960, a composer named Charles Dumont arrived at the posh Paris apartment of Edith Piaf with fear in his heart and songs in his briefcase. At the time, Piaf was perhaps the most famous entertainer in France and one of the best-known singers in the world. She was also quite frail. Although she was just forty-four years old, addiction, accidents, and hard living had ravaged her body. She weighed less than a hundred pounds. Three months earlier Piaf had been in a coma because of liver damage.

Yet despite her wispy presence, she remained notoriously mercurial and hot-tempered. She considered Dumont and his professional partner, lyricist Michel Vaucaire, who had joined him on the visit, second-rate musical talents. Earlier in the day, her secretary had left messages trying to cancel the meeting. Piaf initially refused to see the men, forcing them to wait uneasily in her living room. But just before she went to bed, she appeared, swaddled in a blue dressing gown, and relented.

She'd hear one song, she told them. That's it.

Dumont sat down at Piaf's piano. Sweaty and nervous, he began playing his music while softly speaking the lyrics Vaucaire had written.[1]

> *Non, rien de rien.*
> *Non, je ne regrette rien.*
> No, nothing at all.
> No, I regret nothing at all.

She asked Dumont to play the song again, wondering aloud whether he'd really written it. She assembled a few friends who happened to be visiting to hear it. Then she gathered her household staff for a listen.

Hours passed. Dumont played the song over and over, more than twenty times, according to one account. Piaf telephoned the director of L'Olympia, the premier Parisian concert venue, who arrived just before dawn to hear the work.

> *Non, rien de rien.*
> *Non, je ne regrette rien.*
> *C'est payé, balayé, oublié.*
> *Je me fous du passé.*
> No, nothing at all.
> No, I regret nothing at all.
> It's paid, swept away, forgotten.
> I couldn't care less about the past.

A few weeks later, Piaf sang the two-minute, nineteen-second song on French television. In December, when she performed it as the rousing final number of a concert that helped rescue L'Olympia from financial ruin, she received twenty-two curtain calls. By the end of the following year, fans had purchased more than one million copies of her "Je ne regrette rien" record, elevating her status from chanteuse to icon.

Three years later, Piaf was dead.

One cold Sunday morning in February of 2016, Amber Chase awoke in her apartment in the western Canadian city of Calgary. Her then-boyfriend (and now-husband) was out of town, so the previous evening she had gone out with some girlfriends, a few of whom had slept over. The friends were talking and drinking mimosas when Chase, propelled by some combination of inspiration and boredom, said, "Let's go get tattooed today!" So, they climbed into the car and rolled to Jokers Tattoo & Body Piercing on Highway 1, where the resident artist inked two words on Chase's skin.

The tattoo Chase got that day was nearly identical to the one Mirella Battista decided on five years earlier and 2,400 miles away. Battista grew up in Brazil, and moved to Philadelphia in her early twenties to attend college. She relished her adopted city. While in school, she landed a job at a local accounting firm. She made lots of friends. She even forged a long-term romantic relationship with a Philly guy. The two seemed headed for marriage when, five years into the relationship, she and the boyfriend broke up. So, nine years after arriving in America, and looking for what she called a "reset button," she moved back to Brazil. However, weeks before returning, she had two words tattooed just behind her right ear.

Unbeknownst to Battista, her brother, Germanno Teles, had gotten a nearly identical tattoo the previous year. Teles became enamored of motorcycles as a boy, an affection his safety-conscious physician parents neither shared nor supported. But he learned everything he could about motorcycles, saved his *centavos*, and eventually purchased a Suzuki. He loved it. Then one afternoon while riding on the highway near his Brazilian hometown of Fortaleza, he was hit from the side by another vehicle, injuring his left leg and limiting his future riding days. A short time later, he had the image of a motorcycle tattooed just below the knee of his injured leg. Beside it were two words in script arching alongside the path of his scar.

The tattoo Teles got that day was nearly identical to the one Bruno Santos would get in Lisbon, Portugal, in 2013. Santos is a human resources executive who doesn't know Chase, Battista, or Teles. Frustrated at his job, he walked out of the office one afternoon and headed directly to a tattoo parlor. He emerged with a three-syllable phrase imprinted on his right forearm.

Four people living on three continents, each with tattoos that bear the same two words:

NO REGRETS.

A DELIGHTFUL BUT DANGEROUS DOCTRINE

Some beliefs operate quietly, like existential background music. Others become anthems for a way of living. And few credos blare more loudly than the doctrine that regret is foolish—that it wastes our time and sabotages our well-being. From every corner of the culture the message booms. Forget the past; seize the future. Bypass the bitter; savor the sweet. A good life has a singular focus (forward) and an unwavering valence (positive). Regret perturbs both. It is backward-looking and unpleasant—a toxin in the bloodstream of happiness.

Little wonder, then, that Piaf's song remains a standard across the world and a touchstone for other musicians. Artists who have recorded songs titled "No Regrets" range from jazz legend Ella Fitzgerald to British pop star Robbie Williams to the Cajun band Steve Riley & the Mamou Playboys to American bluesman Tom Rush to Country Music Hall of Fame inductee Emmylou Harris to rapper Eminem. Luxury car brands, chocolate bars, and insurance companies all have championed the philosophy by using Piaf's "Je ne regrette rien" in their television ads.[2]

And what greater commitment to a belief system than to wear it literally on your sleeve—like Bruno Santos, who had the ethic enshrined in black lowercase letters between the elbow and wrist of his right arm?

If thousands of ink-stained body parts don't convince you, listen instead to two giants of American culture who shared neither gender, religion, nor politics but who aligned on this article of faith. Leave "no room for regrets," counseled positive thinking pioneer the Rev. Dr. Norman Vincent Peale, who shaped twentieth-century Christianity and mentored Richard Nixon and Donald Trump. "Waste no time on . . . regret," advised Justice Ruth Bader Ginsburg, the second woman to serve on the U.S. Supreme Court, who practiced Judaism and achieved late-in-life goddess status among American liberals.[3]

Or take the word of celebrities if that's your jam. "I don't believe in regrets," says Angelina Jolie. "I don't believe in regrets," says Bob Dylan. "I don't believe in regrets," says John Travolta. And transgender star Laverne Cox. And fire-coal-walking motivation maestro Tony Robbins. And headbanging Guns N' Roses guitarist Slash.[4] And, I'd bet, roughly half the volumes in the self-help section of your local bookstore. The U.S. Library of Congress contains more than fifty books in its collection with the title *No Regrets*.[5]

Embedded in songs, emblazoned on skin, and embraced by sages, the anti-regret philosophy is so self-evidently true that it's more often asserted than argued. Why invite pain when we can avoid it? Why summon rain clouds when we can bathe in the sunny rays of positivity? Why rue what we did yesterday when we can dream of the limitless possibilities of tomorrow?

This worldview makes intuitive sense. It seems right. It feels convincing. But it has one not insignificant flaw.

It is dead wrong.

What the anti-regret brigades are proposing is not a blueprint for a life well lived. What they are proposing is—forgive the terminology, but the next word is carefully chosen—bullshit.

Regret is not dangerous or abnormal, a deviation from the steady path to happiness. It is healthy and universal, an integral part of being human. Regret is also valuable. It clarifies. It instructs. Done right, it needn't drag us down; it can lift us up.

And that is not some gauzy daydream, a gooey aspiration confected to make us feel warm and cared for in a cold and callous world. That is what scientists have concluded in research that began more than a half century ago.

This is a book about regret—the stomach-churning feeling that the present would be better and the future brighter if only you hadn't chosen so poorly, decided so wrongly, or acted so stupidly in the past. Over the next thirteen chapters, I hope you'll see regret in a fresh and more accurate light, and learn to enlist its shape-shifting powers as a force for good.

We shouldn't doubt the sincerity of people who say they have no regrets. Instead, we should think of them as actors playing a role—and playing it so often and so deeply that they begin to believe the role is real. Such psychological self-trickery is common. Sometimes it can even be healthy. But more often the performance prevents people from doing the difficult work that produces genuine contentment.

Consider Piaf, the consummate performer. She claimed—indeed, proclaimed—that she had no regrets. But a quick review of her forty-seven years on earth reveals a life awash in tragedy and troubles. She bore a child at age seventeen, whom she abandoned to the care of others and who died before turning three. Did she not feel a twinge of regret about that death? She spent one portion of her adult life addicted to alcohol and another addicted to morphine. Did she not regret the dependencies that stifled her talents? She maintained, to put it mildly, a turbulent private life, including a disastrous marriage, a dead lover, and a second husband she saddled with debt. Did she not regret at least some of her romantic choices? It's difficult to picture Piaf on her deathbed celebrating her decisions, especially when many of those decisions sent her to that deathbed decades before her time.

Or take our far-flung tattooed tribe. Talk with them just a little and it's clear that the outer expression of "No regrets"—the performance—and the inner experience diverge. For example, Mirella Battista devoted many years to a serious relationship. When it collapsed, she felt awful. And if she had a chance for a do-over, she likely would have made different choices. That's regret. But she also acknowledged her suboptimal choices and learned from them. "Every single decision brought me to where I am right now and made me who I am," she told me. That's the upside of regret. It's not as if Battista erased regret from her life. (After all, the word is permanently marked on her body.) Nor did she necessarily minimize it. Instead, she optimized it.

Amber Chase, who was thirty-five when we talked over Zoom

one evening, told me, "There's so many wrong turns you can take in life." One of hers was her first marriage. At age twenty-five, she married a man who, it turned out, "had a lot of issues." The union was often unhappy, occasionally tumultuous. One day, with zero notice, her husband disappeared. "He got on a plane and left . . . and I didn't know where he was for two weeks." When he finally called, he told her, "I don't love you anymore. I'm not coming home." In a blink, the marriage was over. If she had to do it over again, would Chase have married the guy? No way. But that unfortunate move propelled her journey to the happy marriage she has today.

Chase's tattoo even winks at the flimsiness of the philosophy it claims to endorse. Hers doesn't say "No Regrets." It says "No Ragrets"—with the second word intentionally misspelled. The choice was an homage to the movie *We're the Millers*, an otherwise forgettable 2013 comedy in which Jason Sudeikis plays David Clark, a small-time marijuana dealer forced to assemble a fake family (a wife and two teenage kids) to work off a debt to a big-time dealer. In one scene, David meets Scottie P., a sketchy young fellow who's arrived on a motorcycle to take David's "daughter" on a date.

Scottie P. wears a cruddy white tank top that reveals several tattoos, including one that runs along his collarbone and reads, in blocky letters, No Ragrets. David sits him down for a quick talk, which begins with a tour of Scottie P.'s tattoos and leads to this exchange:

DAVID

(pointing to the "No Ragrets" tattoo)

What is the one right there?

SCOTTIE P.

Oh, this? That's my credo. No regrets.

DAVID

(his expression skeptical)

How about that. You have no regrets?

SCOTTIE P.

Nope . . .

DAVID

Like . . . not even a single letter?

SCOTTIE P.

No, I can't think of one.

If Scottie P. ever does muster second thoughts about the words encircling his neck, he wouldn't be alone. About one of every five people who get tattoos (presumably including people whose tattoos read "No Regrets") eventually regret their decision, which is why the tattoo removal business is a $100 million-a-year industry in the United States alone.[6] Chase, though, doesn't regret her tattoo, perhaps because most people will never see it. On that cold Calgary Sunday in 2016, she chose to locate her tattoo on her rear end.

THE POSITIVE POWER OF NEGATIVE EMOTIONS

In the early 1950s, a University of Chicago economics graduate student named Harry Markowitz conceived an idea so elementary it now seems obvious—yet so revolutionary it earned him a Nobel Prize.[7] Markowitz's big idea came to be known as "modern portfolio theory." What he figured out—if I may oversimplify in the service of getting on with the story—were the mathematics that underlie the adage "Don't put all your eggs in one basket."

Before Markowitz came along, many investors believed the route to riches was to invest in one or two high-potential stocks. After all, a few stocks often produced humongous returns. Choose those winners and you'd make a fortune. Under this strategy, you'd end up picking lots of duds. But, hey, that's just the way investing worked. It's risky. Markowitz showed that instead of following this recipe, investors could reduce their risk, and still produce healthy gains, by diversifying. Invest in a basket of stocks, not just one. Broaden the bets across a variety of industries. Investors wouldn't win big on every pick, but over time they'd make a lot more money with a lot less risk. If you happen to have any savings parked in index funds or ETFs, modern portfolio theory is the reason why.

Powerful as Markowitz's insight is, we often neglect applying its logic to other parts of our lives. For example, human beings also hold what amounts to a portfolio of emotions. Some of these emotions are positive—for example, love, pride, and awe. Others are negative—sadness, frustration, or shame. In general, we tend to overvalue one category and undervalue the other. Heeding others' advice and our own intuitions, we stuff our portfolios with positive emotions and sell off the negative ones. But this approach to emotions—to jettison the negative and pile on the positive—is as misguided as the approach to investing that prevailed before modern portfolio theory.

Positive emotions are essential, of course. We'd be lost without them. It's important to look on the bright side, to think cheerful thoughts, to detect light in darkness. Optimism is associated with better physical health. Emotions like joy, gratitude, and hope significantly boost our well-being.[8] We need plenty of positive emotions in our portfolio. They should outnumber the negative ones.[9] Yet overweighting our emotional investments with too much positivity brings its own dangers. The imbalance can inhibit learning, stymie growth, and limit our potential.

That's because negative emotions are essential, too. They help us survive. Fear propels us out of a burning building and makes us step gingerly to avoid a snake. Disgust shields us from poisons and makes us recoil from bad behavior. Anger alerts us to threats and provocations from others and sharpens our sense of right and wrong. Too much negative emotion, of course, is debilitating. But too little is also destructive.[10] A partner takes advantage of us again and again; that snake sinks its teeth into our leg. You and I and our upright, bipedal, large-brained sisters and brothers wouldn't be here today if we lacked the capacity, occasionally but systematically, to feel bad.

And when we assemble the full lineup of negative emotions—sadness standing next to contempt perched beside guilt—one emerges as both the most pervasive and most powerful.

Regret.

The purpose of this book is to reclaim regret as an indispensable emotion—and to show you how to use its many strengths to make better decisions, perform better at work and school, and bring greater meaning to your life.

I begin with the reclamation project. In Part One—which comprises this chapter and the next three—I show why regret matters. Much of this analysis taps an extensive body of scholarship that has accumulated over the last several decades. Economists and game theorists, working in the shadow of the Cold War, began studying the topic in the 1950s, when obliterating the planet with a nuclear bomb was the ultimate regrettable act.

Before long, a few renegade psychologists, including the now legendary Daniel Kahneman and Amos Tversky, realized that regret offered a window into not only high-stakes negotiations but the human mind itself. By the 1990s, the field widened further, and a broad group of social, developmental, and cognitive psychologists began investigating the inner workings of regret.

These seventy years of research distill to two simple yet urgent conclusions:

Regret makes us human.

Regret makes us better.

After I've reclaimed regret, I'll move to divulging its contents. Part Two, "Regret Revealed," rests in large part on two extensive research projects of my own. In 2020, working with a small team of survey research experts, we designed and carried out the largest quantitative analysis of American attitudes about regret ever conducted: the American Regret Project. We surveyed the opinion and categorized the regrets of 4,489 people who comprised a representative sample of the U.S. population.* At the same time, we launched a website, the World Regret Survey (www.worldregret survey.com), that has collected more than sixteen thousand regrets from people in 105 countries. I've analyzed the text of those responses and conducted follow-up interviews with more than 100 people who submitted regrets. (On the pages between chapters, as well as in the text itself, you'll hear the voices of participants in the World Regret Survey and peek into every corner of the human experience.)

With these two massive surveys as the base, the seven chapters of Part Two examine what people truly regret. Most academic research on the topic has categorized regrets by the domains of

---

* You can see the full survey and results at www.danpink.com/surveyresults.

people's lives—work, family, health, relationships, finances, and so on. But beneath this surface I found a deep structure of regret that transcends these domains. Nearly all regrets fall into four core categories—foundation regrets, boldness regrets, moral regrets, and connection regrets. This deep structure, previously hidden from view, offers new insights into the human condition as well as a pathway to a good life.

Part Three, "Regret Remade," describes how to turn the negative emotion of regret into a positive instrument for improving your life. You'll learn how to undo and reframe some regrets to adjust the present. You'll also learn a straightforward, three-step process for transforming other regrets in ways that prepare you for the future. And I'll explore how to anticipate regret, a behavioral medicine that can help us make wiser decisions but that should also come with a warning label.

By the time you reach the end of the book, you'll have a new understanding of our most misunderstood emotion, a set of techniques for thriving in a complicated world, and a deeper sense of what makes you tick and what makes life worth living.

"I regret pawning my flute. I loved my flute in high school, but when I got to college and was broke I pawned it for thirty dollars and never had the money to go back and get it. My mother worked so hard to pay for that instrument when I was in beginner band and I loved it so much. It was my prized possession. I know it sounds silly because it's a 'thing,' but it represented so much more—my mother supporting me and making payments on an instrument we couldn't afford, hours and hours of practice learning to play, happy memories with my closest friends in marching band. Losing it is something I can't change and I have a recurring dream about it."

Female, 41, Alabama

//

"I regret rushing to marry my wife. Now, three kids later, it is difficult to go back in time, and divorce would break up and hurt my kids too much."

Male, 32, Israel

//

"When I was a child, my mother would send me to a small local store for a few grocery items. I frequently would steal a candy bar when the grocer wasn't looking. That's bothered me for about sixty years."

Female, 71, New Jersey

2.

Why Regret
Makes Us Human

What is this thing we call regret?

For a sensation so easy to recognize, regret is surprisingly difficult to define. Scientists, theologians, poets, and physicians have all tried. It is "the unpleasant feeling associated with some action or inaction a person has taken which has led to a state of affairs that he or she wishes were different," say the psychotherapists.[1] "Regret is created by a comparison between the actual outcome and that outcome that would have occurred had the decision maker made a different choice," say the management theorists.[2] It is "a feeling of unpleasure associated with a thought of the past, together with the identification of an object and the announcement of an inclination to behave in a certain way in the future," say the philosophers.[3]

If the precise definition feels elusive, the reason is revealing: regret is better understood less as a thing and more as a process.

TIME TRAVELING AND STORYTELLING

This process begins with two abilities—two unique capacities of our minds. We can visit the past and the future in our heads. And we can tell the story of something that never actually happened. Human beings are both seasoned time travelers and skilled fabulists. These two capabilities twine together to form the cognitive double helix that gives life to regret.

Consider this regret, one of the many thousands submitted in the World Regret Survey:

> I wish I had followed my desire to get a graduate degree in my chosen field instead of giving in to my dad's wishes and then dropping out of that program. My life would be on a different trajectory now. It would be more satisfying, fulfilling, and would have given me a greater sense of accomplishment.

In just a few words, this fifty-two-year-old woman from Virginia pulls off a stunning feat of cerebral agility. Discontent with the present, she mentally returns to the past—decades earlier, when she was a young woman contemplating her educational and professional path. Once there, she *negates* what really happened— giving in to her father's wishes. And she substitutes an alternative: she enrolls in the graduate program *she* prefers. Then she hops back in her time machine and hurtles forward. But because she's reconfigured the past, the present she encounters when she arrives is vastly different from the one she left moments earlier. In this newly remodeled world, she's satisfied, fulfilled, and accomplished.

This combination of time travel and fabulism is a human superpower. It's hard to fathom any other species doing something so complex, just as it's difficult to imagine a jellyfish composing a sonnet or a raccoon rewiring a floor lamp.

Yet we deploy this superpower effortlessly. Indeed, it is so deeply imprinted in human beings that the only people who lack the ability are children whose brains haven't fully developed and adults whose brains have been beset by illness or injury.

For example, in one study, developmental psychologists Robert Guttentag and Jennifer Ferrell read a story to a group of children that went something like this:

Two boys, Bob and David, live near each other and ride their bikes to school each morning. To get to school, the boys take a bike path that circles a pond. Bikers can ride around the right side of the pond or the left side. Both paths are the same distance and are equally smooth. Every day, Bob takes the path around the right side of the pond. Every day, David takes the path around the left side of the pond.

One morning, Bob, as usual, rides around the right side of the pond. But overnight, a tree branch has fallen into the path. Bob collides with the branch, falls off his bike, hurts himself, and is late to school. The left side of the path was fine.

That same morning, David, who always takes the left path, decides instead to ride around the right side of the pond. David also hits the branch, is tossed off his bicycle, gets hurt, and arrives late to school.

The researchers then asked the children, "Who would be more upset about deciding to ride along the path that went around the right side of the pond that day?" Bob, who takes that path every day, or David, who usually rides on the left side but today decided to ride on the right side? Or would they feel the same?

The seven-year-olds "performed very similarly to adults on the measures of the understanding of regret," Guttentag and Ferrell write. Seventy-six percent of them understood that David would likely feel worse. But the five-year-olds showed little understanding of the concept. About three-fourths of them said the boys would feel the same.[4] It takes a few years for young brains to acquire the strength and muscularity to perform the mental trapeze act—swinging between past and present and between reality and imagination—that regret demands.[5] That's why most children don't begin to understand regret until age six.[6] But by age eight, they develop the ability even to anticipate regret.[7] And by adolescence, the thinking skills necessary to experience regret have fully emerged.[8] Regret is a marker of a healthy, maturing mind.

It is so fundamental to our development and so critical to proper functioning that, in adults, its absence can signal a grave problem. An important 2004 study makes that plain. A team of cognitive scientists organized a simple gambling game in which participants had to choose one of two computerized roulette-style wheels to spin. Depending on where the arrow landed on their chosen wheel, they would either win money or lose money. When participants spun a wheel and lost money, they felt bad. No surprise. But when they spun a wheel, lost money, and learned that if they'd chosen the other wheel, they'd have *won* money, they felt *really* bad. They experienced regret.

However, one group didn't feel any worse when they discovered that a different choice would have produced a better outcome: people with lesions on a part of the brain called the orbitofrontal cortex. "[T]hey seem to experience no regret whatsoever," neuroscientist Nathalie Camille and her colleagues wrote in the journal *Science*. "These patients fail to grasp this concept."[9] In other words, the inability to feel regret—in some sense, the apotheosis of what the "no regrets" philosophy encourages—wasn't an advantage. It was a sign of brain damage.

The pattern is similar for other diseases of the brain, neuroscientists have found. Several studies present participants with a straightforward test like this:

> Maria gets sick after visiting a restaurant she often visits. Ana gets sick after eating at a restaurant she's never visited before. Who regrets their choice of restaurant more?

Most healthy people immediately know the answer is Ana. But people with Huntington's disease, an inherited neurodegenerative disorder, don't see the obviousness. They just guess; they land on the correct response no more often than chance.[10] It's much the same among people suffering from Parkinson's disease. They, too, fail to deduce the response you probably intuited instantly.[11] The effect is especially devastating for schizophrenia patients. Their illness scrambles the complex thinking I've been describing, creating a reasoning deficit that impairs the ability to comprehend or experience regret.[12] Such deficits are so pronounced in so many psychiatric and neurological diseases that physicians now use this impairment to identify deeper problems.[13] In short, people without regrets aren't paragons of psychological health. They are often people who are seriously ill.

Our twin abilities to travel through time and to rewrite events power the regret process. But the process isn't complete until we take two additional steps that distinguish regret from other negative emotions.

First, we compare. Return to the fifty-two-year-old woman from the survey, the one who wishes she'd followed her own educational desires rather than her father's. Suppose she were suffering simply because her current situation is miserable. That alone doesn't constitute regret. That's sadness, melancholy, or despair. The emotion *becomes* regret only when she does the work of boarding the time machine, negating the past, and *contrasting* her grim actual present with what might have been. Comparison lives at regret's core.

Second, we assess blame. Regret is your own fault, not someone else's. One influential study found that roughly 95 percent of the regrets that people express involve situations they controlled rather than external circumstances.[14] Think again about our regretful Virginian. She compares her unsatisfying situation to an imagined alternative and comes up wanting. That step is necessary, but it's not sufficient. What nudges her fully into the realm of regret is the reason that alternative doesn't exist: her own decisions and actions. She's the cause of her own suffering. That makes regret different—and far more distressing—than a negative emotion like disappointment. For instance, I might feel disappointed that my hometown basketball team, the Washington Wizards, didn't win the NBA championship. But because I neither coach the team nor suit up for games, I'm not responsible and therefore can't regret it. I just sulk and wait until next season. Or consider an example from Janet Landman, a former University of Michigan professor who has written widely about regret. One day, a child loses her third tooth. Before going to sleep, she puts the tooth under her pillow. When she awakens the next morning, she discovers that the Tooth Fairy has forgotten to replace the tooth with a prize. The child is *disappointed*. But it's "the child's parents [who] *regret* the lapse."[15]

Thus we have two abilities that separate humans from other animals, followed by two steps that separate regret from other negative emotions. That is the process that produces this uniquely painful and uniquely human emotion. Although it sounds complicated, the process occurs with little awareness and even less effort. It's part of who we are. As two Dutch scholars, Marcel

Zeelenberg and Rik Pieters, put it, "People's cognitive machinery is preprogrammed for regret."[16]

"AN ESSENTIAL COMPONENT OF THE HUMAN EXPERIENCE"

The result of this cognitive preprograming is that regret, despite all the exhortations to banish it, is remarkably common. In the American Regret Project, we asked our 4,489-person sample a question about their behavior that intentionally avoided using the r-word: *How often do you look back on your life and wish you had done things differently?* The responses, shown in the chart below, are telling.

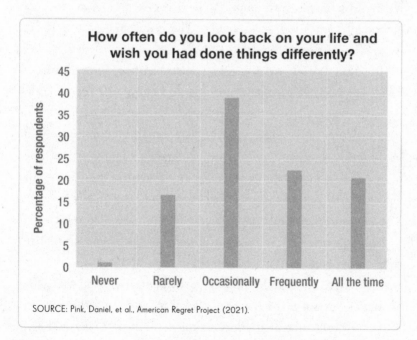

SOURCE: Pink, Daniel, et al., American Regret Project (2021).

Only 1 percent of our respondents said that they never engage in such behavior—and fewer than 17 percent do it rarely.

Meanwhile, about 43 percent report doing it frequently or all the time. In all, a whopping 82 percent say that this activity is at least occasionally part of their lives, making Americans far more likely to experience regret than they are to floss their teeth.[17]

This finding echoes what researchers have been discovering for forty years. In 1984, social scientist Susan Shimanoff recorded the everyday conversations of a collection of undergraduates and of married couples. She analyzed the recordings and transcripts and identified the words that expressed or described emotions. Then she compiled a list of the emotions, positive and negative, that people mentioned most frequently. Feelings like happiness, excitement, anger, surprise, and jealousy all cracked the top twenty. But the most common negative emotion—and the second most common emotion of any kind—was regret. The only emotion mentioned more often than regret was love.[18]

In 2008, social psychologists Colleen Saffrey, Amy Summerville, and Neal Roese examined the prevalence of negative emotions in people's lives. They presented participants with a list of nine such emotions: anger, anxiety, boredom, disappointment, fear, guilt, jealousy, regret, and sadness. Then they asked people a series of questions about the role these feelings played in their lives. The emotion that participants said they experienced the most was regret. The emotion they said they valued the most was also regret.[19]

Subsequent research around the world has produced similar results. A 2016 study that tracked the choices and behavior of more than a hundred Swedes found that participants ended up regretting about 30 percent of the decisions they'd made during the previous week.[20] Another research effort sampled the experiences and attitudes of several hundred Americans. This survey, which I'll examine more fully in Chapter 5, found that regrets were omnipresent and spread across every realm of life, leading the study's authors to declare that regret "constitutes an essential component of the human experience."[21]

In fact, I have yet to uncover a study disconfirming the ubiquity of this emotion. (And believe me, I've looked hard.) Scholars in every field, approaching the subject from different directions and using a variety of methodologies, arrive at the same conclusion: "To live, it seems, is to accumulate at least some regrets."[22]

When Michele Mayo was about to turn fifty, she decided to get a tattoo—something to mark the milestone and affirm her convictions. As she mulled over her decision, she thought back to her childhood. The daughter of an American army officer and a French mother, Mayo spent her early years in Germany, where her father was stationed. During holidays, the family would take long drives to visit her grandmother in the French countryside. On those drives, Mayo, her sisters, and her mom would pass the time by belting out her mother's favorite song.

In 2017, as an early birthday present to herself, she traveled from her home to nearby Salem, Massachusetts, and returned with the skin beneath her right wrist looking like this:

Photo credit: Kathleen Basile

Mayo's mother was an Edith Piaf fan. And the singer's words, which the family sang on those long-ago car trips, stuck with her daughter into adulthood. They embodied "how I live my life, how I felt about my life," Mayo told me. She says she doesn't have regrets. Yet like the others I talked to, she follows that claim by describing blunders she made and the choices she bungled. Like all of us, she's frequently climbed aboard her mental time machine to rewrite a story, comparing what is to what might have been and taking responsibility for the gap. For Mayo, though, the sinking feeling at the end of this chain of thinking, the negative emotion many try to elude, has been valuable. "Those things that I wish I might not have done taught me something about what to do in the future. . . . Even the mistakes I think of as learning experiences," she says. "I hope on my deathbed I can say that."

The five words on her wrist remind her of that aspiration every day. But she's also curious about the singer who made those words famous. "Did you know that she [Edith Piaf] died destitute?" Mayo asks me. "I think about her and wonder, did she really at the end not have any regrets? Imagine if you could interview her now," she says.

Despite the many wonders of video conferencing, I cannot pull off such an interview. But biographers and journalists have provided clues about what Piaf was thinking on October 10, 1963, less than three years after recording the song that would seal her fame. As she lay in bed, life about to slip from her battered forty-seven-year-old body, her final words were, "Every damn thing you do in this life you have to pay for."[23]

Does that sound like a person with no regrets?

However, if Piaf had reckoned with her regrets, if she had

confronted them rather than tried to wriggle past them, she would have discovered something more important: *Every damn thing you do in life can pay off for you.* Because, as we're about to discover, regret doesn't just make us human. It also makes us better.

"I regret nearly every big decision I have ever made. I apparently suck at the big decisions. Little decisions are a snap."

Male, 55, West Virginia

//

"When my husband was hospitalized just before his death, I wanted to climb into the bed next to him to cuddle, but I did not. How I wish I had done that."

Female, 72, Florida

//

"I wish I didn't worry about what other people think. I still struggle with this."

Male, 33, Japan

3.

At Leasts and If Onlys

Of the 306 events at the 2016 Summer Olympics in Rio de Janeiro, the women's individual cycling road race was among the most grueling. The course stretched some 140 kilometers (nearly 87 miles) across city streets and through a national park. It required riders to make several steep climbs, survive one treacherous descent, and negotiate a long patch of cobblestone road. But when the yellow flag dropped at 12:15 p.m. on the first Sunday of August, sixty-eight elite cyclists set off alongside Copacabana Beach for a shot at Olympic glory.

The race lived up to its brutal promise. The temperature hovered in the seventies (the low twenties Celsius) with a punishing 75 percent humidity. The sun frequently broke through the clouds and roasted the pavement. When the sunshine retreated, a light rain misted the course. One rider suffered a savage crash. Others exhausted themselves early. And nearly four hours after the start, with just three kilometers remaining in the race, American Mara Abbott held the lead, followed by a clutch of three riders about twenty-five seconds behind her.

"She's got gold in her hands," said announcer Rochelle Gilmore, who was calling the race for Olympic television.

But Abbott, known more for climbing than for sprinting, couldn't hold on. With just 150 meters left—that is, with 99.9 percent of the race complete—the other three riders pushed past her. Clustered together, they strained for the finish line.

Anna van der Breggen of the Netherlands edged out Emma Johansson of Sweden by the width of a tire. Italy's Elisa Longo Borghini rolled up behind them. All three women had beaten expectations and earned Olympic medals.

Imagine the look on their faces.

No, really. Take a moment and picture their emotions. Visualize what they felt like after years of training and hours of struggle culminated in the ultimate athletic prize.

Since 1872, when Charles Darwin published *The Expression of the Emotions in Man and Animals*, scientists have explored how facial expressions reveal our moods. We often try to conceal our feelings—to display humility instead of pride or resolve instead of heartbreak—but our faces can betray us. And at the podium ceremony following this race, the faces of these Olympic winners disclosed their emotions.

Here, in part of a photo taken by Tim de Waele, is the smiling winner after receiving her gold medal:

Here is the almost equally elated silver medalist:

And here is the pleased—but not totally thrilled—third-place finisher after receiving her bronze:

Even world-class athletes are emotional creatures. And at this epochal moment in their careers, their emotions are unmistakable. The finishers ascend in positivity—happy, happier, happiest.

Faces don't lie.

But authors sometimes do. And I've been lying to you.

Here is de Waele's entire photograph of the 2016 Olympic women's road race podium:

The beaming athlete in the middle is indeed the gold medalist, Anna van der Breggen. But the very happy woman to her left (and your right) is Elisa Longo Borghini, the Italian rider who finished third. The least gleeful of the trio is silver medalist Emma Johansson.

In other words, the person with the worst of the three outcomes (Borghini) looks happier than one of the people who beat her (Johansson). And this is not some aberrant photo, even though there are images of Johansson smiling that day. Consider the athletes' reactions immediately after they crossed the finish line. Gold medalist van der Breggen raised both arms in triumph. Bronze medalist Borghini began high-fiving an invisible partner. Silver medalist Johansson buried her head in her hands. Nor is the emotional contrast the result of failed expectations. Borghini came into the race ranked higher than Johansson and expected to do better.

What you see on these Olympian faces is instead a phenomenon that behavioral scientists identified more than twenty-five years ago that opens another window into understanding regret.

THE THRILL OF DEFEAT AND THE AGONY OF VICTORY

The human superpower I described in Chapter 2—our ability to mentally travel through time and to conjure incidents and outcomes that never happened—enables what logicians call "counterfactual thinking." Split the adjective in two and its meaning is evident. We can concoct events that run *counter* to the actual *facts*. "Counterfactuals are . . . a signature example of the imagination and creativity that stand at the intersection of thinking and feeling," say Neal Roese of Northwestern University and Kai Epstude of the University of Groningen, two leading scholars of the subject.[1] Counterfactuals permit us to imagine what might have been.

One of the clearest demonstrations of their impact comes from the Olympics. In a now famous study of the 1992 Summer Games in Barcelona, Victoria Medvec and Thomas Gilovich of Cornell University and Scott Madey of the University of Toledo collected videos of about three dozen silver and bronze medalists. They presented the videos to a group of participants who didn't know much about sports and hadn't paid attention to the games. Participants observed the athletes, but not during competitions. They watched them—with the final results hidden—in the immediate aftermath of their events and on the medal podium. Then they rated the competitors' facial expressions on a ten-point "agony-to-ecstasy" scale that I've reproduced below:

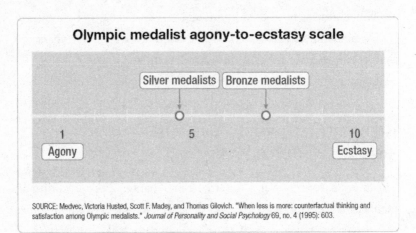

Olympic medalist agony-to-ecstasy scale

Silver medalists — Bronze medalists

1 — Agony   5   10 — Ecstasy

SOURCE: Medvec, Victoria Husted, Scott F. Madey, and Thomas Gilovich. "When less is more: counterfactual thinking and satisfaction among Olympic medalists." *Journal of Personality and Social Psychology* 69, no. 4 (1995): 603.

The athletes who finished third appeared significantly happier than those who finished second. The average rating of the facial expressions of bronze medalists was 7.1. But silver medalists—people who'd just placed second in the most elite competition in the world—were neutral, even tilting slightly toward unhappy. Their rating: 4.8.

The reason, researchers concluded, was counterfactual thinking.

Counterfactuals can point in either of two directions—down or up. With "downward counterfactuals," we contemplate how an alternative could have been *worse*. They prompt us to say "At least . . ."—as in, "Sure, I got a C+ on that exam, but at least I passed the course and don't have to take it again." Let's call these types of counterfactuals *At Leasts*.

The other variety are known as "upward counterfactuals." With upward counterfactuals, we imagine how things could have gone *better*. They make us say "If only . . ."—as in, "If only I'd attended class more often and done all the reading, I'd have gotten a much better grade." Let's call these counterfactuals *If Onlys*.

When researchers reviewed competitors' post-event television interviews, they found the bronze medalists happily humming *At Leasts*. "At least I didn't finish fourth. At least I got a medal!" Silver medalists, though, were wracked with *If Onlys*. And that hurt. "Second place is only one step away from the cherished gold medal and all of its attendant social and financial rewards," Medvec and her colleagues wrote. "Thus, whatever joy the silver medalist may feel is often tempered by tortuous thoughts of what might have been had she only lengthened her stride, adjusted her breathing, pointed her toes, and so on."[2]

The idea that people who finish higher feel worse is provocative—the sort of alluring discovery that captures headlines and enraptures social media. For the last decade, social science has contended with what some have called a "replication crisis."[3] Many findings, especially those that seem most surprising and newsworthy, don't hold up on closer examination. When other scholars rerun the experiments, they often don't produce the same tantalizing results, calling into question the validity of the earlier findings.

But the Medvec-Gilovich-Madey study has been replicated. Even its replications have been replicated. For example, David Matsumoto of San Francisco State University assembled about 21,000 photographs from the men's and women's judo competitions at the 2004 Olympic Games in Athens, a massive photo set that represented 84 athletes from 35 countries. Regardless of the national origin or ethnicity of the athletes, the difference in facial expression among the medalists was striking. During the podium ceremonies, the gold medalists were almost all smiling widely (what's called a "Duchenne smile"). So, too, were most of the bronze medalists. The silver medalists? Not so much. They smiled only one-fourth as much as their counterparts.[4]

In 2020, William Hedgcock of the University of Minnesota and Andrea Luangrath and Raelyn Webster of the University of Iowa went further. They collected photos of 413 athletes from 142 sports and 67 countries over five separate Olympic Games. But instead of asking other people to evaluate the athletes' facial expressions, as in previous studies, they used Emotient, computer software that encodes facial expressions automatically. (The program allowed researchers to scrutinize more expressions more quickly, free of any potential bias from human examiners.) Once again, the results held. Gold medalists smiled the most. But bronze medalists smiled much more than silver medalists. "[T]hose who were objectively better off nonetheless felt worse," the paper's authors noted.[5]

I've watched that 2016 Rio road race several times. In the minutes after it ended, it's easy to see the solace of *At Least* and the sting of *If Only*. Borghini, the bronze medalist, looked jubilant. She hopped off her bike, loped toward a group of friends and family, and embraced each one. "Elisa Borghini is absolutely delighted with a medal at the Olympic Games!" the announcers cried.

Johansson, meanwhile, huddled quietly with her husband, her affect flat, as the announcers offered their own upward counterfactual. "Another fifty or one hundred meters, and she might have got out over the top," they speculated. It was a moment of "mixed emotions" for her, they explained. "A silver medalist once again." Indeed, Johansson had won the silver in the same event during the 2008 Olympics. (She didn't compete in the 2012 games because of an injury.) She'd finished second in several other races, too, earning her a nickname in the cycling world that she never embraced—Silver Emma. "She's 'Silver Emma,'" Johansson's mother told Swedish television after the finish. "I think she's happy, but she wanted gold."[6]

If only.

THE PARADOX OF PAIN AND THE PAIN OF PARADOX

At Leasts make us feel better. "At least I ended up with a medal—unlike that American rider who blew it in the final seconds of the race and never reached the podium." "I didn't get that promotion, but at least I wasn't fired." *At Leasts* deliver comfort and consolation.

If Onlys, by contrast, make us feel worse. "If only I'd begun that final chase two seconds earlier, I'd have won a gold medal." "If only I'd taken a few more stretch assignments, I'd have gotten that promotion." *If Onlys* deliver discomfort and distress.

It would seem, therefore, that we humans would favor the first category—that we'd choose the warmth of *At Least* over the chill of *If Only*. After all, we're built to seek pleasure and to avoid pain—to prefer chocolate cupcakes to caterpillar smoothies and sex with our partner to an audit with the tax man.

But the truth is different. You're much more likely to have a Silver Emma moment than a Bronze Borghini one. When researchers have tracked people's thoughts by asking them to keep daily diaries or by pinging them randomly to ask what's on their mind, they've discovered that *If Onlys* outnumber *At Leasts* in people's lives—often by a wide margin.[7] One study found that 80 percent of the counterfactuals people generate are *If Onlys*. Other research puts the figure even higher.[8] The main exception are situations in which we've eluded calamity. For instance, one study of tourists who witnessed a deadly tsunami but managed to escape found that, several months later, they generated ten *At Least* comparisons for every *If Only*. These people didn't feel aggrieved for being exposed to a natural disaster; they felt lucky for surviving it.[9] In a sense, that's also the experience of the bronze medalists, who avoided the far less devastating catastrophe of being denied an Olympic medal. But in our day-to-day experiences, those quotidian moments that form most of human existence, we're much more likely to conjure *If Onlys* when we ponder what might have been. That's how our brains and minds work.

Two decades of research on counterfactual thinking exposes an oddity: thoughts about the past that make us feel better are relatively rare, while thoughts that make us feel worse are exceedingly common. Are we all self-sabotaging masochists?

No—or at least not all of us. Instead, we are organisms programmed for survival. *At Least* counterfactuals preserve our feelings in the moment, but they rarely enhance our decisions or performance in the future. *If Only* counterfactuals degrade our feelings now, but—and this is key—they can improve our lives later.

Regret is the quintessential upward counterfactual—the ultimate *If Only*. The source of its power, scientists are discovering, is that it muddles the conventional pain-pleasure calculus.[10] Its very purpose is to make us feel worse—because by making us feel worse today, regret helps us do better tomorrow.

"I regret being embarrassed about being Mexican. I was able to pass (I'm light-skinned), so many people didn't know I was Mexican until they met my family (who were dark). I have now come to embrace my race and heritage. I'm just ashamed I didn't do it sooner."

Female, 50, California

//

"I regret cheating on my boyfriend of seven years instead of just breaking up with him. Then I regret doing it again after he agreed to stay together."

Female, 29, Arizona

//

"My deepest regret of my fifty-two years of life is having lived it fearfully. I have been afraid of failing and looking foolish, and as a result I did not do so many things that I wish I had done."

Male, 52, South Africa

4.

Why Regret Makes Us Better

"There is a crack, a crack in everything
That's how the light gets in."

Leonard Cohen, 1992

erhaps you're familiar with the First Law of Holes: "When you find yourself in a hole, stop digging." And perhaps you've ignored this law. We often compound bad choices by continuing to invest time, money, and effort in losing causes instead of stanching our losses and switching tactics. We increase funding in a hopeless project because we've spent so much already. We redouble efforts to salvage an irredeemable relationship because we've already devoted a few years to it. The psychological concept is known as "escalation of commitment to a failing course of action." It's one of the many cognitive biases that can pollute our decisions.

It's also something that experiencing regret can fix. Gillian Ku, now of London Business School, found that getting people to think about a previous escalation of commitment, and then to regret it, decreased their likelihood of making the error again.[1]

Inducing this unpleasant feeling of *If Only* improved their future behavior.

THE THREE BENEFITS OF REGRET

Reducing cognitive biases like escalation of commitment to a failing course of action is just one way that regret, by making us feel worse, can help us do better. A look at the research shows that regret, handled correctly, offers three broad benefits. It can sharpen our decision-making skills. It can elevate our performance on a range of tasks. And it can strengthen our sense of meaning and connectedness.

1. Regret can improve decisions.

To begin understanding regret's ameliorative properties, imagine the following scenario.

During the pandemic of 2020–21, you hastily purchased a guitar, but you never got around to playing it. Now it's taking up space in your apartment—and you could use a little cash. So, you decide to sell it.

As luck would have it, your neighbor Maria is in the market for a used guitar. She asks how much you want for your instrument.

Suppose you bought the guitar for $500. (It's acoustic.) No way you can charge Maria that much for a used item. It would be great to get $300, but that seems steep. So, you suggest $225 with the plan to settle for $200.

When Maria hears your $225 price, she accepts instantly, then hands you your money.

Are you feeling regret?

Probably. Many people do, even more so in situations with stakes greater than the sale of a used guitar. When others accept our first offer without hesitation or pushback, we often kick ourselves for not asking for more.[2] However, acknowledging one's regrets in such situations—inviting, rather than repelling, this aversive emotion—can improve our decisions in the future. For example, in 2002, Adam Galinsky, now at Columbia University, and three other social psychologists studied negotiators who'd had their first offer accepted. They asked these negotiators to rate how much better they could have done if only they'd made a higher offer. The more they regretted their decision, the more time they spent preparing for a subsequent negotiation.[3] A related study by Galinsky, University of California, Berkeley's, Laura Kray, and Ohio University's Keith Markman found that when people look back at previous negotiations and think about what they regretted not doing—for example, not extending a strong first offer—they made better decisions in later negotiations. What's more, these regret-enhanced decisions spread the benefits widely. During their subsequent encounters, regretful negotiators expanded the size of the pie and secured themselves a larger slice. The very act of contemplating what they hadn't done previously widened the possibilities of what they could do next and provided a script for future interactions.[4]

The main effect, several studies show, is on our "decision hygiene."[5] Leaning into regret improves our decision-making process—because the stab of negativity slows us down. We collect more information. We consider a wider range of options. We take more time to reach a conclusion. Because we step more carefully, we're less likely to fall through cognitive trapdoors like confirmation bias.[6] One study of CEOs found that encouraging business leaders to reflect on their regrets exerted a "positive influence on their future decisions."[7]

Barry Schwartz, one of the first social psychologists to take regret seriously, explains that this unpleasant feeling "serves several important functions." Regret can "emphasize the mistakes we made in arriving at a decision, so that, should a similar situation arise in the future, we won't make the same mistakes."[8]

This theme ran through many of the entries in the World Regret Survey, including this one from a parent with a long memory:

> I yelled at my daughter when she was five, on the way to school, when she spilled some yogurt on her uniform. I really laid into her and I have regretted it ever since. She didn't deserve that. I upset her so much, and for what? A bit of a stain on her uniform? I will never stop regretting that moment. I have never yelled at her in that way again. So I learned from that mistake, but I wish I could take that moment back.

This parent still feels bad about past behavior, but has used that feeling to make different decisions going forward and never scream at the child that way again.

While some of us parents are still trying to improve our decision-making, the capacity for regret might be a fundamental part of how our sons and daughters learn to reason and make decisions themselves. Irish researchers, across several experiments, have shown that children's decision-making capabilities improve tremendously once they cross the developmental threshold, around age seven, that allows them to experience regret. "The development of regret allows children to learn from previous decisions in order to adaptively switch their choices," write Eimear O'Connor, Teresa McCormack, and Aidan Feeney.[9]

Our cognitive apparatus is designed, at least in part, to sustain us in the long term rather than balm us in the near term. We need the ability to regret our poor decisions—to feel bad about them—precisely so we can improve those decisions in the future.

2. Regret can boost performance.

Clairvoyants smash egg pools.

That's an anagram for *Psychologists love anagrams*. And it's true. Anagrams are a staple of psychological research. Usher participants into a room. Give them some words or phrases to rearrange into other words or phrases. Then manipulate their mood, their mindset, their environment, or any other variable to see how it affects their performance.

For example, in one experiment, Keith Markman (from one of the negotiation studies) and two colleagues gave participants ten anagrams to solve. After supposedly "grading" the results, they told participants that they'd found only half of the available words. Then they poked people with a little regret. "Close your eyes and think about your actual performance on the anagrams compared to how you might have performed better," they told the participants. "Take a minute and vividly evaluate your performance in comparison to how you might have performed better." Their heads now swimming with *If Onlys*, these puzzle-solvers felt worse—especially compared to another group that had been asked to make *At Least* comparisons. But on the next round, the regretful group solved more puzzles and stuck with the task longer than anyone else in the experiment.[10] This is one of the central findings on regret: it can deepen persistence, which almost always elevates performance. One of the pioneers in studying counterfactual thinking, Neal Roese, whose research appears throughout these pages and the

Notes, used anagrams in one of his earliest and most influential papers. He, too, found that inducing regret—poking participants with *If Onlys*—enabled people to solve more anagrams and to solve them faster.[11]

Or leave the laboratory and enter the casino. One intriguing experiment, also led by Markman, asked people to play blackjack against a computer. The experimenters told half the participants that after the first round, they'd depart. They told the other half that after the first round, they'd play a few more hands. People who knew they'd be playing again generated many more *If Onlys* than people who were one-and-done. They were more likely to regret pursuing a flawed card-playing strategy or taking too much or too little risk. The first group, meanwhile, avoided negativity. They mostly generated *At Leasts* ("At least I didn't lose all my money!"). But the card players in the second group willingly initiated the unpleasant process of experiencing regret "because they needed preparative information to help them perform better," the researchers wrote. "Participants who did not expect to play again needed no such information and, instead, wanted only to feel good about their current performance."[12]

Even thinking about *other* people's regrets may confer a performance boost. Several studies have introduced a character named Jane, who's attending a concert of her favorite rock band. Jane begins the concert in her ticketed seat, but then moves to another seat to be closer to the stage. A bit later, the band announces that promoters will soon randomly select a seat and give a free trip to Hawaii to whoever is sitting in it. Sometimes participants in this experiment hear that the seat that Jane recently *switched to* is the one that wins the free trip. Rejoice! Other times participants hear that the seat that Jane *left* is the one that wins. Regret! People who heard Jane's *If Only* saga, and then took a section of the Law

School Admission Test, scored 10 percent higher than a control group. They also did a better job of solving complex puzzles like the Duncker candle problem, a famous experimental test of creative thinking.[13] Getting people to think counterfactually, to experience even vicarious regret, seems to "crack open the door to possibilities," Galinsky (from the negotiation studies) and Gordon Moskowitz explain. It infused people's subsequent deliberations with more strength, speed, and creativity.

To be sure, regret doesn't always elevate performance. Lingering on a regret for too long, or replaying the failure over and over in your head, can have the opposite effect. Selecting the wrong target for your regret—say, that you wore a red baseball cap at the blackjack table rather than that you took another card when you were holding a ten and a king—offers no improvement. And sometimes the initial pain can momentarily throw us. But most times, reflecting even a bit on how we might benefit from a regret boosts our subsequent showing.[14]

Feelings of regret spurred by setbacks might even be good for your career. A 2019 study by the Kellogg School of Management's Yang Wang, Benjamin Jones, and Dashun Wang looked at a fifteen-year database of applications that junior scientists had submitted for a prestigious National Institutes of Health grant. The study authors selected more than a thousand applications that hovered near the rating threshold necessary to win the grant. About half the applicants just cleared the threshold. They got the grant, eked out a narrow win, and eluded regret. The other half fell just short. These applicants missed the grant, endured a narrow miss, and suffered regret. Then the researchers examined what happened to these scientists' careers. People in the narrow-miss *If Only* group systematically outperformed those in the narrow-win *At Least* group in the long run. These Silver Emmas of science

were subsequently cited much more often, and they were 21 percent more likely to produce a hit paper. The researchers concluded
that it was the setback itself that supplied the fuel. The near miss
likely prompted regret, which spurred reflection, which revised
strategy, which improved performance.[15]

3. Regret can deepen meaning.

A few decades ago, I spent four years in Evanston, Illinois, where
I earned an undergraduate degree from Northwestern University.
I'm generally happy with my college experience. I learned a ton
and made several lifelong friends. But I've occasionally wondered
what my life would have been like had I not been able to go to
college or if I'd attended another university. And for some strange
reason, those musings usually make me more, not less, satisfied
with the experience, as if this small slice of time was somehow
integral to the full story of my life.

Turns out, I'm not that special.

In 2010, a team of social scientists that included Kray, Galinsky,
and Roese asked a collection of Northwestern undergraduates to
reflect counterfactually about their choice of college and their
choice of friends during college. When the students engaged in this
sort of thinking, imagining they'd attended a different university
or fallen in with a different set of pals, their reaction was like mine.
The actual choice somehow felt more significant. "Counterfactual
reflection endows both major life experiences and relationships with
greater meaning," the Northwestern study concluded.

And this effect isn't limited to periods when we're young and
self-absorbed. In fact, other research has found that people who
thought counterfactually about pivotal moments in their life experienced greater meaning than people who thought explicitly

about the meaning of those events. The indirect paths of *If Only* and *At Least* offered a faster route to meaning than the direct path of pondering meaning itself.[16] Likewise, when people consider counterfactual alternatives to life events, they experience higher levels of religious feeling and a deeper sense of purpose than when they simply recount the facts of those events.[17] This way of thinking can even increase feelings of patriotism and commitment to one's organization.[18]

While these studies examined the broader category of counterfactuals, regret in particular deepens our sense of meaning, and steers our lives toward its pursuit. For instance, conducting a "mid-life review" focused on regrets can prompt us to revise our life goals and aim to live afresh.[19] Or take Abby Henderson, a twenty-nine-year-old behavioral health researcher, who contributed to the World Regret Survey:*

> I regret not taking advantage of spending time with my grandparents as a child. I resented their presence in my home and their desire to connect with me, and now I'd do anything to get that time back.

Henderson grew up, the youngest of three siblings, in a happy home in Phoenix, Arizona. Her paternal grandparents lived in the small town of Hartford City, Indiana. Just about every winter, to escape the Midwest cold, they'd visit for a month or two, usually staying in the Henderson house. Young Abby was not into it. She was a quiet kid whose parents both worked, so she relished the time after school when she could hang out at home by herself. Her grandparents disturbed that peace. Her grandmother, waiting for

---

* Respondents to the World Regret Survey submitted their regrets anonymously. But they could volunteer their email address if they were willing to be contacted for a follow-up interview.

her when she returned from classes, always wanted to hear about her day—and Abby resisted the attempts at connection.

Now she regrets it.

"The biggest regret is that I didn't hear their stories," she told me in an interview. But that has altered her approach to her own parents. Sparked by this regret, she and her siblings bought their father, who's in his seventies, a subscription to StoryWorth. Each week the service sends an email that contains a single question (What was your mother like? What is your fondest childhood memory? And—yes—what regrets do you have?). The recipient responds with a story. At the end of the year, those stories are compiled into a hardcover book. Because of the poke of *If Only*, she said, "I seek out more meaning. I seek out more connection. . . . I don't want to feel the way when my parents die that I felt about my grandparents of 'What did I miss?'"

Abby says this ache helped her to see her own life as a puzzle with meaning as the centerpiece. "When people around me say 'No regrets,' I push back and say, 'If you don't make mistakes, how are you going to learn and grow?'" she told me. "I mean, who makes it through their twenties without regrets? The bad jobs I took, the bad dates I went on." But she eventually discovered that every time she had a regret, "it was in part because I was trying to remove meaning from the equation."

One of the traits Abby remembers about her grandmother was her otherworldly baking skills, especially the pies she regularly served for dessert. "If all you've ever had is flavorless pie, you're going to think pies are 'meh.' But once you've had my grandma's strawberry pie, there is no going back." For Abby, there's a metaphor lurking in that baking tin.

"My life is more flavorful because of my regrets," she told me. "I remember the bitterness of the taste of regret. So when something is sweet, good god, it's so much sweeter." She knows she'll never get the time back with her grandparents. "It's a flavor that will always be missing," she says. Collecting the stories of her father, which she wouldn't have done without the prod of *If Only*, helps. "It is a beautiful substitute," she says.

"But it isn't a replacement. Nothing will fill in that flavor. I will spend the rest of my life with a little bit of a gap. But that's going to inform everything else that I do."

When we handle it properly, regret can make us better. Understanding its effects hones our decisions, boosts our performance, and bestows a deeper sense of meaning. The problem, though, is that we often don't handle it properly.

WHAT ARE FEELINGS FOR?

At some point in its pages, nearly every popular book about human behavior wheels out William James, the nineteenth-century American polymath and Harvard professor who wrote the first psychology textbook, taught the first psychology course, and is widely considered to be the founding parent of the field. This book will now honor that tradition.

In chapter 22 of his 1890 masterwork *The Principles of Psychology*, James contemplated the purpose of the human ability to think. He proposed that how we think, even *what* we think, depends on our situation. "Now that I am writing, it is essential that I conceive my paper as a surface for inscription," he wrote. "If I failed to do that I should have to stop my work." But in other situations—suppose he needed to light a fire and nothing else was available—he'd think of the paper differently. The paper itself has infinite variations—"a combustible, a writing surface, a thin thing, a hydrocarbonaceous thing, a thing eight inches one way and ten another, a thing just one furlong east of a certain stone in my neighbor's field, an American thing, etc., etc., *ad infinitum.*"

Then he dropped an intellectual grenade that reverberates still today: "My thinking is first and last and always for the sake of my doing."[20]

Modern psychologists have affirmed James's observation, while shaving off ten words in the service of pith: *Thinking is for doing.*[21] We act in order to survive. We think in order to act.

But feelings are more complicated. What is the purpose of emotions—especially unpleasant emotions like regret? If thinking is for doing, what is feeling for?

One view: **Feeling is for ignoring.** Emotions aren't significant, this perspective holds. They're mere annoyances, distractions from serious matters. Better to bat them away or cast them into oblivion. Focus on the hardheaded, eschew the softhearted, and you'll be fine.

Alas, stashing negativity in your emotional basement merely delays the moment when you must open the door and face the mess you've stored inside. Blocked emotions, writes one therapist, can even lead to "physical problems like heart disease, intestinal problems, headaches, insomnia and autoimmune disorders."[22] Burying negative emotions doesn't dissipate them. It intensifies them, and the contaminants leach into the ground soil of our lives. Consistently diminishing negative emotions isn't a sound strategy either. It risks turning you into Professor Pangloss from *Candide*, who when dealt one catastrophe after another simply declares, "All for the best in the best of all possible worlds." Minimizing techniques like *At Least* counterfactuals do have their place, as I'll explain in Chapter 12. They can soothe us, and sometimes we need soothing. But they can also supply us with false comfort and strip us of the tools to address cold reality, becoming a downward-facing dogma that undermines decisions and blunts growth.

Another view: **Feeling is for feeling.** According to this position, emotions are the essence of our being. Talk about them. Vent about them. Luxuriate in them. "Always trust your feelings," this perspective says.[23] They are to be honored—sat upon a throne and revered. Emotions are the one real truth. They are all there is; all the rest is commentary.

For negative emotions, especially regret, this approach is even more perilous than the Panglossian strategy of delusion-through-elusion. Too much regret is dangerous, sometimes devastating. It can lead to rumination, which severely degrades well-being, and to the regurgitation of past mistakes, which can inhibit forward progress. Excessive regret is linked to an array of mental health problems—most prominently depression and anxiety, but also post-traumatic stress disorder.[24] "Individuals who ruminate on their regrets are more likely to report reduced life satisfaction and to experience difficulty coping with negative life events," concludes one paper.[25] This is especially true when regrets become repetitive. Repetitive thought can worsen regret, and regret can exacerbate repetitive thought, creating a descending spiral of pain.[26] Rumination doesn't clarify and instruct. It muddies and distracts. When feeling is only for feeling, we build a chamber from which it's difficult to escape.

When it comes to regret, a third view is healthier: **Feeling is for thinking.** Don't dodge emotions. Don't wallow in them either. Confront them. Use them as a catalyst for future behavior. If thinking is for doing, feeling can help us think.[27]

This approach to regret is akin to the modern science of stress.

Stress. It sounds bad. But stress, we now know, is not a single, unmalleable entity. Much of how it affects us, even what it fundamentally is, depends on our individual mindset.[28] If we think of stress as permanent and debilitating, that tugs us in one direction. If we think of it as temporary and enhancing, that leads us in a different direction. Chronic, omnipresent stress is poisonous. But occasional, acute stress is helpful, even essential.

Regret can work in a similar way. For example, framing regret as a judgment of our underlying character—who we are—can be destructive. Framing it as an evaluation of a particular behavior in a particular situation—what we did—can be instructive. Suppose you forgot a loved one's birthday. A regret about being a clueless, uncaring person won't help. A regret about not keeping important dates in one's computer calendar or not regularly expressing gratitude to relatives is useful. Ample research shows that people who accept, rather than judge, their negative experiences end up faring better.[29]

Likewise, framing regret as an opportunity rather than a threat helps us transform it—so that it operates as a sharp stick rather than a leaden blanket. Regrets that hurt deeply but dissolve quickly lead to more effective problem solving and sturdier emotional health.[30] When regret smothers, it can weigh us down. But when it pokes, it can lift us up.

The key is to use regret to catalyze a chain reaction: the heart signals the head, the head initiates action. All regrets aggravate. Productive regrets aggravate, then activate. The chart on the next page explains the process. It also demonstrates the key point: your response determines your result. When you feel the spear of regret, you have three possible responses. You can conclude that feeling is for ignoring—and bury or minimize it. That leads to delusion. You can conclude that feeling is for feeling—and wallow in it. That leads to despair. Or you can conclude that feeling is for thinking—and address it. What does this regret tell you? What instructions does it offer for making better decisions? For improving your performance? For deepening your sense of meaning?

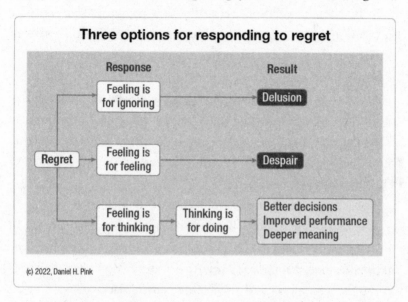

Three options for responding to regret

(c) 2022, Daniel H. Pink

When feeling is for thinking, and thinking is for doing, regret is for making us better.

In the fifteenth century, or so the story goes, a Japanese shogun named Ashikaga Yoshimasa dropped a Chinese tea bowl, which broke into several pieces when it hit the floor. He sent the damaged bowl back to China to be repaired. But what he received in return months later was an ungainly mess of an object, the bowl's pieces held together by bulky metal staples. There's got to be a better way, he thought, and he asked local craftspeople to find it.

They chose to repair the pottery by sanding down the edges of the broken pieces and gluing them back together using lacquer mixed with gold. The artisans' goal wasn't to faithfully reproduce the original work, or even to conceal its newly acquired flaws. It was to transform the piece into something better. Their work established a new—and now centuries-old—art form called *kintsugi*. "By the 17th century," according to one report, "kintsugi was such a fashionable phenomenon that some people were known to smash their tea bowls on purpose in order to embed them with golden-veined repairs."[31]

Kintsugi (which translates to "golden joinery") considers the breaks and the subsequent repairs part of the vessel's history, fundamental elements of its being. The bowls aren't beautiful despite the imperfections. They're beautiful because of the imperfections. The cracks make them better.

What's true for ceramics can also be true for people.

Just ask Mara Abbott. If you can't quite place the name, I'll refresh your memory. In the 2016 Olympic road race I described in the previous chapter, she's the American rider who lost the lead in the final moments and finished in fourth place.

"The days that followed the race were some of the largest experiences of heartbreak that I've ever felt," she told me via Zoom one February afternoon from Buffalo, Wyoming, where she now works as a newspaper reporter. The word she chooses to capture the experience: "shattering."

Yet she reassembled the pieces and found new insights in the fissures. The Rio contest was the last race of a successful ten-year cycling career. The experience didn't improve her times or earn her another trophy. But "it somehow gave me this touchstone and perspective that makes other decisions and value judgments easier for me," she said. Most of all, she yearns to recapture the experience of being as fully engaged and alive as she was on that August afternoon. "The opportunity and the feeling that I got out of that loss, and that fullness and that wholeness, is the greatest privilege I could have ever asked for." Because of the pain, she sees the rest of her life with greater urgency and purpose. "If you have a broken heart, it means you have done something big enough and important enough and valuable enough to have broken your heart."

As Mara Abbott suggests, the cracks are how the light gets in. And as we'll see in the next section, peering through those cracks offers a glimpse of the good life.

Part Two

REGRET
REVEALED

//

"Me arrepiento no haber cambiado mis hábitos alimenticios desde joven, fume y he consumido mucho alcohol. También consumía carne los tres tiempos de comida casi mi vida entera. Hace seis meses cambie a un estilo de vida vegano y me he sentido mejor que nunca antes en mi vida, solo me pongo a pensar si hubiera hecho esto desde joven."*

Male, 46, Honduras

//

"I spent too much time trying to meet others' idea of normal. Accept yourself, love your neighbor, and make each day a special memory."

Nonbinary, 62, Utah

//

"My biggest regret is not using my time as a stay-at-home mom to really teach my children about their relationship with God and Jesus Christ. I could have used my time with them better to help them develop and strengthen their faith, which in turn would have given them the best foundation to succeed in life."

Female, 54, Minnesota

---

* "I regret that I didn't change my eating habits during my youth and that I smoked and drank a lot of alcohol. I also ate meat three meals (a day) for most of my life. Six months ago, I became a vegan and I've never felt better in my life. I just wonder how things could have been if I'd done this when I was young."

5.

Regret on the Surface

"my body is NOT a temple it's a STORAGE
UNIT for my REGRETS."

@ElyKreimendahl, Twitter, 2020

What do people regret?

That's a question that pollsters and professors have been asking since the middle of the twentieth century. In 1949, for instance, George Gallup, founder of the American Institute of Public Opinion, surveyed U.S. citizens about what they considered to be the biggest mistake of their lives. The number one answer was a resounding "Don't know."

Four years later, Gallup returned with what is likely the first polling question directly about regret. "Generally speaking," his team asked in 1953, "if you could live your life over again, would you live it in much the same way as you have, or would you live it differently?" A majority of Americans, as you see from the headline on the following page, said they wouldn't change a thing.

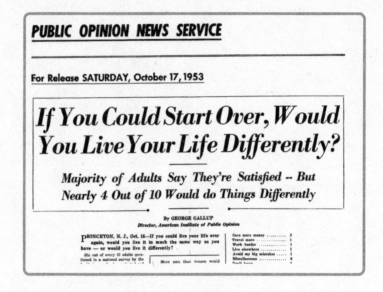

PUBLIC OPINION NEWS SERVICE

For Release SATURDAY, October 17, 1953

If You Could Start Over, Would You Live Your Life Differently?

Majority of Adults Say They're Satisfied -- But Nearly 4 Out of 10 Would do Things Differently

By GEORGE GALLUP
Director, American Institute of Public Opinion

PRINCETON, N. J., Oct. 16—If you could live your life over again, would you live it in much the same way as you have — or would you live it differently?

Six out of every 10 adults questioned in a national survey by the

More men than women would

Save more money	2
Travel more	1
Work harder	1
Live elsewhere	1
Avoid my big mistakes	1
Miscellaneous	6

This discomfort with admitting and enumerating hardship makes sense. Think about life in 1953. World War II lingered in the public memory. The United Kingdom, with a newly crowned twenty-seven-year-old queen, was still rationing food. Japan and much of Europe were digging out of devastation. It was the year Joseph Stalin died, the Korean War ended, and the first polio vaccine was developed. With the exterior world so fraught, interior contemplation might have felt indulgent. Navel-gazing was still a few years from becoming a national pastime.

Yet peeking through the unease was a theme that researchers would slowly come to endorse. In the 1949 poll, the runner-up to "Don't know" for biggest mistake was "Didn't get enough education." In the 1953 poll, among those who had regrets, the top choice, selected by 15 percent of the sample, was "Get more education." That, too, makes sense. In 1953, just 6 percent of the U.S. population had attended four or more years of college. More than half of Americans had not completed high school.[1] *Brown v. Board of Education*, the U.S. Supreme Court case that declared segregated public schools a violation of the Constitution, was still a year away. More Americans were beginning to imagine the possibilities of education in the future, which perhaps meant that more regretted not having or pursuing those possibilities in the past. By 1965, when Gallup conducted a poll for *Look* magazine about what Americans would do differently if they had a chance to relive their lives, 43 percent chose "Get more education," nearly three times what respondents said eight years earlier.[2]

Over the ensuing decades, pollsters became less interested in regret, but academics assumed the mantle. In the 1980s, Janet Landman and Jean Manis of the University of Michigan examined the regrets of a collection of both female undergraduates and adult women who'd visited the university's career center. The top regrets of each group landed squarely in the realm of education. For the older women, *If Only* thoughts typically involved curtailing their studies too early.[3] In 1989, Arlene Metha and Richard Kinnier of Arizona State University surveyed the major regrets of women in three age cohorts—those in their twenties, people between ages thirty-five and fifty-five, and those sixty-four and older. Across all three groups, the top regret they chose was "I would have taken my education more seriously and worked harder on it."[4] A different set of Arizona State researchers surveyed community college students a few years later and found similar results. "Educational/academic" regrets were most frequent.[5] In 1992, Mary Kay DeGenova, a family studies scholar, surveyed retired people and found that among the domains of friends, family, work, education, religion, leisure, and health, the most common regret was education.[6]

On it went. At Cornell University, Victoria Medvec and Thomas Gilovich, who conducted the famous Olympic medal study I described in Chapter 3, in 1994 asked an assortment of people about their regrets. Education—both "missed educational opportunities" and "bad educational choice"—came out on top. (Personal relationships—"missed romantic opportunity" and "unwise romantic adventure"—finished next.)[7] The following year, Medvec and Gilovich joined Nina Hattiangadi to study the regrets of seventy-somethings who as children had been identified as high-IQ prodigies. Once again, education topped their list—including regrets about wasting time in college, choosing the wrong field of study, and not completing enough schooling.[8]

In 2005, Neal Roese and Amy Summerville decided to round up the existing research to determine with greater certainty which "domains in life produce the greatest potential for regret." Their meta-analytic summary examined nine previous studies, including

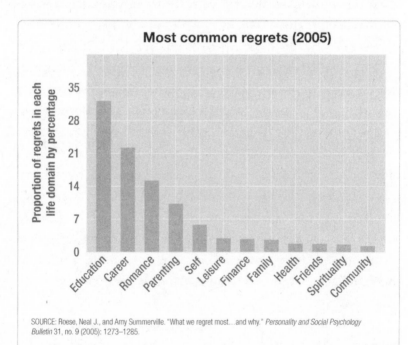

Most common regrets (2005)

Proportion of regrets in each life domain by percentage

Education, Career, Romance, Parenting, Self, Leisure, Finance, Family, Health, Friends, Spirituality, Community

SOURCE: Roese, Neal J., and Amy Summerville. "What we regret most...and why." *Personality and Social Psychology Bulletin* 31, no. 9 (2005): 1273–1285.

the ones I mentioned above, and established twelve categories of regret—for example, career ("If only I were a dentist"), romance ("I wish I'd married Jake instead of Edward"), and parenting ("If only I'd spent more time with my kids"). Education again came out on top. Thirty-two percent of the 3,041 participants in the studies they analyzed selected it as their prime regret.

"Education is the number one regret at least in part because in contemporary society, new and further education of one sort or another is available to nearly all individuals," they concluded. If you didn't finish college, you might be able to return. If you needed additional training or skills, the right courses might be available. If you didn't earn a graduate degree in your twenties, maybe you can pursue one in your forties or fifties. "Opportunity breeds regret," they wrote, and "education is open to continual modification throughout life."[9]

Roese and Summerville titled their paper "What We Regret Most . . . and Why." And its conclusion seemed straightforward. But this analysis didn't settle the issue. They and other researchers soon discovered that their answer to the "what" was faulty—and that their answer to the "why" revealed something deeper than they realized.

WHAT DO PEOPLE *REALLY* REGRET?

The studies that concluded that education was our greatest regret, despite passing peer review, were pocked with flaws. For instance, most of them took place on college campuses, where concerns about degrees, majors, and curriculum pervade conversation. If the surveys had been conducted in, say, hospitals, pharmacies, or doctors' offices, perhaps health regrets would have dominated.

More important, as Roese and Summerville note, the previous research relied on "samples of convenience" rather than representative slices of the total population. In one study, researchers asked graduate students to hand out questionnaires to people they knew, not exactly the gold standard for random sampling. The study of retired people surveyed 122 older adults living near Purdue University—even though it's unlikely that as western Indiana goes, so goes the rest of the world. In another study, the interviewees were a bricolage of ten emeritus professors, eleven nursing home residents, forty undergraduate students, and sixteen clerical and custodial staff. Roese and Summerville noted that 73 percent of the total sample in their meta-analysis were women, hardly the gender ratio that statistics best practices demand. An overwhelming number of the people surveyed were White. Even the Gallup polls, which were more representative of the U.S. population, often produced less than definitive results. In the 1953 poll, 15 percent of people chose education as their single biggest regret. But an even larger portion—about 40 percent—gave more than one answer to the question.

What was needed, Roese and Summerville concluded toward the end of their paper, was a survey that represented the diversity and complexity of the entire country. And in 2011, Roese and his colleague Mike Morrison took up the challenge. They reached beyond the college campus with a telephone poll of 370 people from across America. Random digit dialing ensured the sample didn't skew toward any single region or demographic group. They asked their participants to report one significant regret in detail, which a team of independent raters then assigned to one of twelve life domains. It was "the first truly representative portrait of where in life the typical American has their biggest regrets," Roese and Morrison wrote.

The portrait they offered—titled "Regrets of the Typical American: Findings from a Nationally Representative Sample"—looked quite different from what had come before. The regrets were widely distributed across several areas of life, with no single category capturing more than 20 percent of the public mind. Regrets involving romance—lost loves and unfulfilling relationships—were the most common, comprising about 19 percent of the total regrets. Family finished next with 17 percent. Education and career each garnered 14 percent.[10]

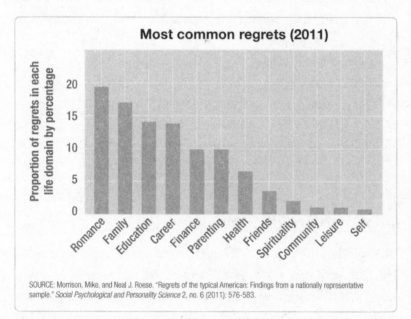

SOURCE: Morrison, Mike, and Neal J. Roese. "Regrets of the typical American: Findings from a nationally representative sample." Social Psychological and Personality Science 2, no. 6 (2011): 576-583.

This more diverse sample also allowed researchers to derive other insights. For example, women were more likely than men to have romance and family regrets. People with the least formal education were more likely to have education regrets, while single, unattached people harbored more romance regrets.

The reasons also veered from previous findings. Once again, the researchers concluded that regret hinged on opportunity. However, while the earlier study suggested that regret lurked in realms where people perceived *lots* of opportunities, this study found the opposite. Areas where the opportunities had vanished—for instance, considering oneself too old for additional education—produced the most regrets. Such low-opportunity regrets (in which a problem could not be fixed) outnumbered high-opportunity regrets (in which a problem could be fixed) by a solid margin.

So, more than a half century after scholars and surveyors began probing individuals about their regrets, they had some answers to their two core questions.

What do people regret?

Lots of stuff.

Why do they have those regrets?

Something about opportunity.

The outcome remained intriguing, but unsatisfying.

OKAY, ONE MORE TIME

The world of survey research has changed considerably since 1953. For that very first regret poll, Gallup and his team interviewed about 1,500 people—often in person—and tabulated the responses without the assistance of even a mainframe computer. Today, my three-year-old smartphone packs more power than the computing might of all the world's universities in the 1950s. And the laptop on which I'm writing this sentence connects me to billions of people across the globe and houses on its hard drive free, open-source software that can analyze massive amounts of data with such speed and ease it would astonish mid-twentieth-century statisticians.

I'm no George Gallup. But today's tools are so powerful, and the costs are dropping so quickly, that even an amateur like me can follow his lead. So, nagged by the sense that we still didn't truly understand what people regret, I tried to find out myself. Working with a large software and data analytics company, which itself contracted with firms that assemble panels of participants, we created the largest and most representative American survey on regret ever attempted—the American Regret Project. We polled 4,489 adults—whose gender, age, race, marital status, geography, income, and education level reflected the composition of the entire U.S. population.

The survey, a full version of which you can find online (www.danpink.com/surveyresults) asked participants seven demographic questions and eighteen research questions—including the big one:

> Regrets are part of life. We all have something we wish we had done differently—or some action we wish we had taken or not taken.
>
> Please look back on your life for a moment. Then describe in 2 or 3 sentences one significant regret you have.

Thousands upon thousands of regrets came spilling into our database. We asked people to place their regret into one of eight categories: career, family (parents, children, grandchildren), partners (spouses, significant others), education, health, finances, friends, something else. And we posed several other questions, many of which you'll read about later in the book.

In our survey, family took the top spot. Nearly 22 percent of respondents voiced a regret in this category, followed closely by the 19 percent whose regret involved partners. Running just behind, and bunched together tightly, were education, career, and finance regrets. Health and friends regrets rounded out the list.

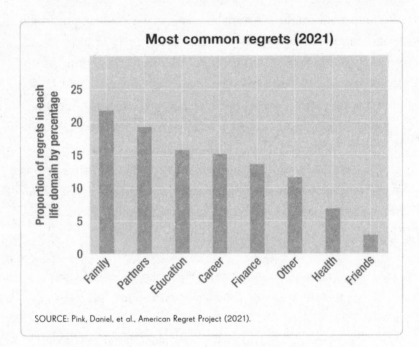

Most common regrets (2021)

SOURCE: Pink, Daniel, et al., American Regret Project (2021).

In other words, the largest and most representative survey of regret ever conducted reached a clear conclusion: American regrets span a wide range of domains rather than cluster into any single category. People do indeed regret a lot of stuff—family relationships, romantic choices, career moves, educational paths, and more.

Maybe that shouldn't surprise us. After all, regret is universal. It's a fundamental part of being human. Human life spreads across multiple domains—we're parents, sons, daughters, spouses, partners, employees, bosses, students, spenders, investors, citizens, friends, and more. Why wouldn't regret straddle domains, too?

What's more, regret makes us better. It sharpens decisions, boosts performance, and deepens meaning. Why would its benefits *not* reach across life domains?

Yet even this outcome remains unsatisfying. It offered a glimmer of understanding, but not nearly the illumination I was seeking. And as I returned to the data, and collected thousands more entries worldwide in the World Regret Survey, I discovered the reason. The question was sound. I was just looking for the answer in the wrong place.

"I didn't practice or 'give it my all' while playing high school basketball. I think it's because I was afraid of being compared and then being worse than my brother—which ultimately happened because of my lack of effort."

Male, 24, Utah

//

"Pretending to be less smart and inventive than I actually am, simply to please/not upset others. This also includes business meetings with clients and then later hearing, 'She's useless in client meetings.'"

Female, 39, Saudi Arabia

//

"I regret not learning more, sooner, about racism."

Female, 78, Pennsylvania

6.

The Four Core Regrets

Kevin Wang has an education regret. In 2013, when he was a senior biology major at Johns Hopkins University, he planned to become a doctor—just like all four of his grandparents. His grades were strong. The only step that remained was the Medical College Admission Test (MCAT). But, as Kevin explained almost a decade later, he procrastinated "so badly on studying for my MCAT that I bombed the test and ended up not getting into medical school." Today, he works in a New York City hospital, but as an administrator who monitors costs rather than a physician who sees patients.

On the other side of the United States, in Southern California, John Welches also has an education regret:

> As I neared the end of completing my BA in creative writing, my professors urged me to apply for an MFA. They said

my writing was strong and would benefit from that level of focus. I'd even won the two fiction awards put out by the program.

The problem: I was getting married a month before graduation. What does a newlywed do after graduating college? Gets a job.

So, instead of heeding his genuine interests and his mentors' counsel, he skipped the master's program, "slunk my way into bank work," and landed a "soul-sucking" job as a copywriter.

Two American men harboring the same regret—a graduate education they didn't pursue for a career they don't have. But how similar, really, are they?

Kevin regrets not taking his future seriously. John regrets not taking a risk. Kevin regrets not meeting other people's expectations. John regrets not setting the right expectations for himself. Kevin regrets a failure to be conscientious. John regrets a failure to be bold. On the surface, their regrets occupy similar terrain. Below the surface, the roots diverge.

Sometimes when I was analyzing entries in the World Regret Survey, I felt less like I was studying our most misunderstood emotion and more like I was operating a gigantic online confessional.

For instance, hundreds of people offered a partner regret like one that came from a sixty-one-year-old man in Australia:

> Being unfaithful to my wife and justifying it selfishly by convincing myself she was the problem is my biggest regret.

A few weeks after that submission arrived, a thirty-seven-year-old Canadian man described a regret about how he once treated his peers:

> I regret bullying a few different kids in my grade growing up. When I think back on it, I cringe and I can't help but wish for a chance to go back and change it.

A short time after that, another thirty-seven-year-old man, this one from California, revealed:

> I cheated in a student election by tossing out a vote from my opponent's friend, who I knew had only come to the meeting to vote for his buddy. I don't think I even needed to do that in order to win, which made compromising my integrity that much sadder.

Three men with regrets that span a wide swath of territory—an Australian marriage, a Canadian childhood, a California election. But how different, really, are they?

All involve a moral breach. At a moment in their lives now stamped in memory, all three faced a choice: Honor their principles or betray them? And at that moment, all three chose wrongly. On the surface, their regrets poke through different patches of life's landscape. Below the surface, they grow from common roots.

SIMILARITY AND DIFFERENCE

If you've ever traveled to a place where people speak a language different from your own, you might have felt a twinge of envy when you encountered a four-year-old. I know that's happened to me.

I began trying to learn Spanish as an adult. It was not *bonita*. I mangled irregular verbs. I mixed up genders and misplaced adjectives. And the subjunctive? *¡Dios mío!* Yet whenever I saw preschoolers in a Spanish-speaking community in the United States or abroad, their speech appeared effortless.

The work of Noam Chomsky helped me understand why. Until the late 1950s, most scientists believed that children were linguistic blank slates who learned language mostly by repeating adults. When children's mimicry was accurate, they'd be praised. When it was off, they'd be corrected. And over time, this process would etch onto their little brains the circuitry of whatever language their parents spoke. The wide variety of tongues spoken around the world testified to this truth. Yes, some languages—Danish and German, for example—shared a history. But language itself lacked a single common foundation.

Beginning with a 1957 book called *Syntactic Structures*, Chomsky capsized these beliefs. He argued that every language was built atop a "deep structure"—a universal framework of rules lodged in the human brain.[1] When children learn to speak, they're not simply parroting sounds. They're activating grammatical wiring that already exists. Language wasn't an acquired skill, Chomsky said. It was an innate capacity. A child learning to speak Vietnamese or learning to speak Croatian is not much different from a child learning to walk in Hanoi or learning to walk in Zagreb. They're just doing what humans do. Yes, individual languages differ—but only in their "surface structures." Hindi, Polish, and Swahili are individual variants on a single template. Underpinning them all is the same deep structure.

Chomsky's idea revolutionized the study of linguistics and expanded our understanding of the brain and mind. He acquired a few detractors over his career, including some who rejected his left-wing politics. But his contribution to science is as undeniable as it is enduring. And one consequence of his work was the realization that among the languages of the world, similarity often conceals difference and difference often conceals similarity.

To cite one of Chomsky's most famous examples,[2] these two English sentences seem nearly identical:

John is eager to please.
John is easy to please.

They both contain five words—a noun, followed by a verb, followed by an adjective, followed by an infinitive. Four of the words are the same; the other varies only by a few letters. But one layer down, the sentences are quite different. In the first, John is the subject. In the second, John is the object. If we restate the second sentence as "It is easy to please John," the meaning holds. But if we restate the first sentence as "It is eager to please John," the meaning crumbles. Their surface structures are the same, but that doesn't tell us much, because their deep structures diverge.

Meanwhile, these two sentences seem different:

Ha-yoon went to the store.
하윤이는 그 가게에 갔다.

But one layer down, they're identical—a noun phrase (*Ha-yoon,* 하윤이는), a verb phrase (*went,* 갔다), and a prepositional phrase (*to the store,* 그 가게에). Their surface structures differ, but their deep structures are the same.

Chomsky demonstrated that what appeared complicated and disorderly wasn't the full story; beneath the Tower of Babel cacophony ran a common human melody.

It took me a while to figure out, but I've discovered that regret, too, has both a surface structure and a deep structure. What's visible and easy to describe—the realms of life such as family, education, and work—is far less significant than a hidden architecture of human motivation and aspiration that lies beneath it.

THE DEEP STRUCTURE OF REGRET

Reading and rereading thousands of regrets is daunting; categorizing and recategorizing them even more so. But as I plowed back through the entries, I began identifying certain words and phrases that kept appearing with no noticeable correlation to the respondent's age, location, gender, or the topic that person was describing.

> "Diligent" . . . "More stable" . . . "Bad habits"
> "Take a chance" . . . "Assert myself" . . . "Explore"
> "Wrong" . . . "Not right" . . . "Knew I shouldn't"
> "Missed" . . . "More time" . . . "Love"

Words and phrases like these offer clues to the deep structure. And as they piled up, like thousands of dots of color in a pointillist painting, they began to take shape. The shapes span the lives of all of us and infiltrate every aspect of how we think, feel, and live. They divide into four categories of human regret.

Foundation regrets. The first deep structure category cuts across nearly all the surface categories. Many of our education, finance, and health regrets are actually different outward expressions of the same core regret: our failure to be responsible, conscientious, or prudent. Our lives require some basic level of stability. Without a measure of physical well-being and material security, other goals become difficult to imagine and even harder to pursue. Yet sometimes our individual choices undermine this long-term need. We shirk in school and leave before we should. We overspend and undersave. We adopt unhealthy habits. When such decisions eventually cause the platform of our lives to wobble, and our futures to not live up to our hopes, regret follows.

Boldness regrets. A stable platform for our lives is necessary, but not sufficient. One of the most robust findings, in the academic research and my own, is that over time we are much more likely to regret the chances we *didn't* take than the chances we did. Again, the surface domain—whether the risk involved our education, our work, or our love lives—doesn't matter much. What haunts us is the inaction itself. Forgone opportunities to leave our hometown or launch a business or chase a true love or see the world all linger in the same way.

Moral regrets. Most of us want to be good people. Yet we often face choices that tempt us to take the low road. When we travel that path, we don't always feel bad immediately. (Rationalization is such a powerful mental weapon it should require a background check.) But over time, these morally dubious decisions can gnaw at us. And, once again, the realm in which they occur—deceiving a spouse, cheating on a test, swindling a business partner—is less significant than the act itself. When we behave poorly, or compromise our belief in our own goodness, regret can build and then persist.

Connection regrets. Our actions give our lives direction. But other people give those lives purpose. A massive number of human regrets stem from our failure to recognize and honor this principle. Fractured or unrealized relationships with spouses, partners, parents, children, siblings, friends, classmates, and colleagues constitute the largest deep structure category of regret. Connection regrets arise any time we neglect the people who help establish our own sense of wholeness. When those relationships fray or disappear or never develop, we feel an abiding loss.

The next four chapters will explore each of these deep structure regrets. You'll hear people around the world describing foundation, boldness, moral, and connection regrets. But as the chorus of voices builds, if you listen carefully, you'll also hear something else: the vivid harmony of what we need to lead a fulfilling life.

"I regret not standing up to the men who raped me. Now that I am stronger both mentally and physically I will never let a man hurt me like that again."

Female, 19, Texas

//

"In 1964, I was invited to join Mississippi Freedom Summer by a college classmate. I took a job with my father's boss in Oklahoma City instead."

Male, 76, California

//

"Following a career path for money instead of for my passion or work I would actually enjoy. My mother convinced me I would starve to death if I pursued a career in art, so now I am stuck behind a desk tangled in management red tape and the life is draining out of me."

Female, 45, Minnesota

7.

Foundation Regrets

A few days after he graduated from high school in 1996, Jason Drent landed a full-time job as a sales associate at Best Buy, the large electronics retailer. Jason's work ethic was ferocious, and his industriousness soon paid off. He quickly became the youngest sales manager in Best Buy history. A few years later, another retailer snatched him away, and Jason scaled the ranks of that company. District manager. Regional manager. Before long, he was earning a six-figure salary and shouldering executive responsibility. He began a series of career-enhancing moves from Ohio to Illinois to Massachusetts to Michigan to Tennessee. Today, at age forty-three, he heads employee relations at the corporate headquarters of a large apparel chain.

By all appearances, Jason Drent is a success story—a young man who endured a difficult childhood, including a stint at a group home, but whose brains, ambition, and grit fueled his ascent in corporate America. But his story, which he told in the World Regret Survey, comes with an important footnote:

I regret not saving money diligently ever since I started working. It's nearly crushing every day to think about how hard I've worked for the last twenty-five years or so, but financially I have nothing to show for it.

Jason has a sterling résumé, but barely a dime in the bank—a positive record of achievement, but a negative net worth.

From his first paycheck at Best Buy, he vowed to himself, "I'm going to buy whatever I want as soon as I can." He wasn't especially extravagant. "It was a lot of nonsensical day-to-day stuff," he told me. A decent car. Some clothing. "The big man on campus" pride, as he described it, of always picking up the tab at restaurant dinners with friends. It felt good.

But the small, daily choices that once beguiled him now haunt him. "It's kind of sad looking back," he told me. "I should have more resources at this point."

For a guy whom antiquity scholars say might never have existed, Aesop has enjoyed a pretty good run as an author. The fables that bear his name (but are likely the product of many creators over many years) date to five centuries before the Common Era. They've been bestsellers for more than two thousand years—fixtures of bookstore children's sections and bedtime story sessions. They remain popular even in the age of podcasts and streaming services, because who among us does not enjoy hearing life lessons delivered by talking animals?

Among the best-known of Aesop's fables is "The Ant and the Grasshopper." The story is deceptively simple. During a long summer, the grasshopper lolls about, plays the fiddle, and tries to entice its friend the ant to join in dancing and other insect debauchery.

The ant declines. It chooses instead the more arduous task of lugging corn and grain into storage.

When winter arrives, the grasshopper realizes its error. It clutches its fiddle for warmth, but soon dies of hunger. The ant and its family, meanwhile, eat well and happily from the store of food that this more forward-thinking creature has collected during the summer.

During one of my conversations with Jason, I told him he reminded me of the grasshopper. He shook his head ruefully. "I never took steps to prepare," he said. During the summer of his life, there were "a lot of cavalier moments where I enjoyed saying 'So what?' and just rolling through it." But in the end, he said, it "was twenty-five years of fiddling."

The first of the four categories in the deep structure of regret are what I call "foundation regrets."

Foundation regrets arise from our failures of foresight and

conscientiousness. Like all deep structure regrets, they start with a choice. At some early moment, we face a series of decisions. One set represents the path of the ant. These choices require short-term sacrifice, but in the service of a long-term payoff. The other choices represent the path of the grasshopper. This route demands little exertion or assiduousness in the short run, but risks exacting a cost in the long run.

At that juncture, we choose the path of the grasshopper.

We spend too much and save too little. We drink and carouse at the expense of exercising regularly and eating right. We apply minimal and grudging effort in school, at home, or on the job. The full ramifications of these incremental choices don't materialize immediately. But over time, they slowly accrue. Soon the full consequences become too towering to deny—and, eventually, too massive to repair.

Foundation regrets sound like this: *If only I'd done the work.*

THE LURE AND THE LOGIC

Foundation regrets begin with an irresistible lure and end with an inexorable logic. Take this Canadian woman, who hails from Alberta but whose regret comes straight out of Aesop:

> I regret not looking after my health through the years. I did lots to hurt my health and not much to help it. Also, I did not save for retirement, and now I'm sixty-two, unhealthy, and broke.

We typically read "The Ant and the Grasshopper" as a morality tale, but it's also a story about cognition. By partying all summer instead of gathering food for the winter, the grasshopper succumbed to what economists call "temporal discounting."[1] He overvalued the now—and undervalued (that is, discounted) the later. When this bias grips our thinking, we often make regrettable decisions.

Aesop's preferred explanatory tool was the parable, but we can convey the point with equal clarity using a simple chart:

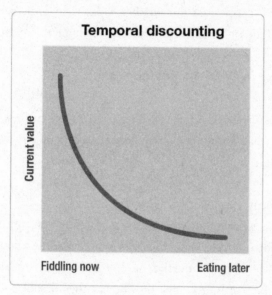

The grasshopper prized fiddling in the moment more than eating in the future. The Alberta woman valued gratification in youth more than health and satisfaction in maturity. Jason Drent says his early paychecks made him feel so "invincible" that they blinded his view into the distance.

In both the American Regret Project and the World Regret Survey, respondents described their experience of temporal discounting with the language of early excess. A thirty-one-year-old man from Arkansas said:

> I drank way too much in my early twenties. Got a DWI. Derailed my plans to join the military.

A forty-five-year-old woman in Ireland:

> I didn't look after myself when I was younger. I drank and smoked too much and slept with too many guys.

A forty-nine-year-old Virginia man:

> I regret that I did not take my college years more seriously. Rather than thinking of the future, I spent too much time enjoying the present.

To identify a foundation regret in yourself or in others, listen for the words "too much"—whether they attach to consuming alcohol, playing video games, watching television, spending money, or any other activity whose immediate lure exceeds its lasting value. Then listen for the words "too little"—whether they describe studying in school, setting aside cash, practicing a sport or musical instrument, or any other undertaking that requires steady commitment. One study of college athletes, for example, found that their greatest regrets centered on too much eating and too little sleep and training.[2]

Temporal discounting is only the beginning, because this deep structure category involves a second time-based issue. Some regrets deliver their pain immediately. If I race my car down the street well above the speed limit and collide with another vehicle, the consequences of the decision, and therefore my regret, are instantaneous. A totaled vehicle, an aching back, a lost day. But foundation regrets don't arrive with the sound and fury of a collision. They proceed at a different pace.

In chapter 13 of Ernest Hemingway's 1926 novel *The Sun Also Rises*, a few of protagonist Jake Barnes's expatriate friends arrive in Pamplona, Spain, and meet for a drink. During the conversation, Mike Campbell, a Scotsman, discloses his recent bankruptcy.

"How did you go bankrupt?" American Bill Gorton asks him.

"Two ways," Campbell replies. "Gradually and then suddenly."[3]

That's also how people discover their foundation regrets. Many individual health, education, or financial missteps are not themselves immediately devastating. But the slowly building force of all those poor decisions can arrive like a tornado—gradually and then suddenly. By the time we realize what's happening, there's not much we can do.

Once again, people used similar language to describe regrets whose consequences they understood too late. A sixty-one-year-old Florida man, unintentionally channeling Hemingway's laconic style, wrote:

Not saving money from an earlier age. Compound interest.

A forty-six-year-old Australian said:

I should have selected different subjects and worked harder earlier in my life to obtain the compounding benefits throughout life.

A thirty-three-year-old Michigan man:

I regret that I didn't appreciate reading earlier in life. Now I see the value of reading and often wonder what the compounding effect would have been if I had started ten to fifteen years earlier.

Compounding. It's a powerful concept, but one our grasshopper minds struggle to comprehend.

Suppose I offered you a choice—$1 million in cash today or one penny that will double in value every day for a month. Most people, experimental evidence shows, would opt for the million bucks.[4] And during the first three and a half weeks of our pact, that decision would seem wise. But after just a little more time—on day thirty—that penny would become more than $5 million. We can explain the power of compounding with another chart, which you'll notice is essentially the mirror image of its predecessor.

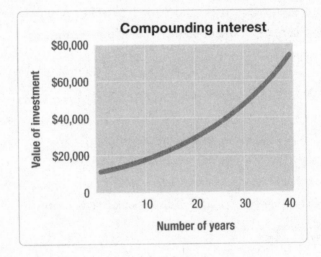

If you invest $10,000 at a 5 percent compounding interest rate, you'll have an extra $500 after one year. After ten years, you'll have made nearly $6,500. After twenty years, you'll almost triple your money. But after thirty years, your stake will be worth over $44,600—more than quadruple what you started with. In the short run, the interest on money you've borrowed or saved doesn't add up to much. In the medium run, it accelerates. In the long run, it explodes. And the principle applies well beyond finance—because small choices about eating, exercising, studying, reading, and working produce explosive benefits or harms over time.

Our brains therefore play a double trick on us. They entice us into valuing the now too much and the later too little. Then they prevent us from understanding the nonlinear, compounding effects of our choice. Overlay the two charts, and they form a trap that can be difficult to escape.

Foundation regrets are not just difficult to avoid. They are also difficult to undo. That is especially the case for financial regrets like Jason's, which people described in vivid terms. A fifty-five-year-old California woman said the debt she's amassed from short-sighted money choices "entangles my feet." For a forty-six-year-old Indian man, lacking a financial foundation prevented him from "having the space to live life." "The money I could have saved makes me a bit sick to my stomach when I think about what I wasted," said a forty-seven-year-old female from Washington State. And a forty-six-year-old woman from Massachusetts who didn't learn "how to manage money better, sooner" concluded that "most of my other regrets all seem to lead back to that one."

Foundation regrets were evenly spread across geography and gender. But they were slightly more prevalent among older respondents, because weaknesses in one's foundation take time to develop and recognize. Said a Tennessee man:

I should have worked harder in college. Achieving better grades would have allowed me to get a better job, earning more, sooner in my career.

At age nineteen, this man's foundation seemed sound. At age twenty-nine, it creaked. At age thirty-nine, it wobbled. Now, at age forty-nine, it feels like it's disintegrating. His footing is shaky because of a set of seemingly small decisions he made three long decades ago. But even younger people, who hadn't yet witnessed the results of their mistakes compound, shared this category of regrets. "I wish I would have studied harder," said a twenty-five-year-old Malaysian woman. "I wish I had worked harder in college and spent my time more judiciously," said another twenty-five-year-old woman, who lives in India.

Many respondents lamented not only the practical ramifications of not tending to one's foundation, but also a more wistful sense of lost opportunity. A forty-nine-year-old woman, more than two decades removed from college, wrote:

I wish I had appreciated the privilege I had to be able to go to university and had worked harder to get a better degree.

The pattern is similar for health decisions—including poor eating habits and lack of exercise—which also gather force and imperil people's foundations. In the World Regret Survey, regrets about tobacco use, particularly starting at a young age, came from respondents on six continents—including this thirty-nine-year-old man from Colombia:

I regret I smoked so much in my life, even though I clearly knew how bad for my health and surroundings this was. I kept smoking a pack a day, sometimes more. I escaped my frustrations and anxiety by smoking cigarettes.

On mental health, foundation regrets often involve a failure to recognize the problem and seek a remedy. As a forty-three-year-old Oregon man put it:

> I regret that I didn't take my mental health seriously in my twenties and, in doing so, utterly lost my sense of self-worth.

Many people who did take steps to rebuild a collapsing psychological foundation regretted not beginning the process sooner. For example, a forty-four-year-old Arizona woman said:

> I regret not finding a good therapist ten or fifteen years earlier.

And a fifty-seven-year-old nonbinary person in Oregon regretted:

> Not taking antidepressants in 2002 when first prescribed, and waiting until 2010. They have been a godsend, and I regret that those eight years could have been so much different had I started earlier.

Embedded in each of these regrets is a solution. Just as foundation regrets can be defined with a well-worn fable, one response to them is contained in a hoary Chinese proverb:

The best time to plant a tree is twenty years ago.

The second-best time is today.

FOUNDATION ATTRIBUTION ERROR

Foundation regrets are trickier than the other three deep structure regrets I'll describe in upcoming chapters. Remember that what distinguishes regret from disappointment is personal responsibility. Disappointments exist outside of your control. The child who wakes up to discover that the Tooth Fairy hasn't left her a reward is *disappointed*. Regrets, in contrast, are your fault. The parents who awaken and realize they forgot to remove their child's tooth and replace it with a reward are *regretful*. But when it comes to matters like physical health, educational attainment, and financial security, the border between personal responsibility and external circumstance is murky.

Are you overweight because of your poor nutritional choices or because nobody ever taught you, let alone modeled, healthy eating? Do you have a meager retirement account because you spent too much on frivolities or because you started your career burdened with student debt and lacking even a thin financial cushion? Did you drop out of college because of your faulty work ethic or because your mediocre secondary school didn't prepare you for the rigors of university classes?

One of the most prevalent cognitive biases—in some ways the über-bias—is called the "fundamental attribution error." When people, especially Westerners, try to explain someone's behavior, we too often attribute the behavior to the person's personality and disposition rather than to the person's situation and context.[5] So, to use a classic example, when another driver cuts us off on the highway, we immediately assume the person is a jerk. We never consider that the person might be speeding to the hospital. Or when someone seems uneasy while giving a presentation, we assume that he's an inherently nervous person rather than someone who doesn't have much experience in front of a crowd. We load too much explanatory freight onto the person and too little onto the situation.

With this category of regrets, something similar might be happening—a *foundation attribution error.* We attribute these failures, in ourselves and others, to personal choices when they're often at least partly the result of circumstances we can't control.* That means that the fix for foundation regrets, and a way to avoid them, is not only to change the person, but to reconfigure that person's situation, setting, and environment. We must create the conditions at every level—society, community, and family—to improve individuals' foundational choices.

Which is what Jason Drent is trying to do.

LESSONS FROM A GRASSHOPPER

In his current job, Jason oversees workplace policies and programs for a retailer that employs more than a thousand associates, many of them young. He approaches the position with a greater sense of mission than he did back when he was a teenager peddling DVD players at Best Buy. "I help them navigate a lot of the basics in life. I'm not the only one with a less-than-great foundation," he said.

He explains to the associates the importance of building their skills and connections and, yes, putting aside a little from every paycheck for the future. He tells them to plan, then tries to show them how—all while attempting to heed the advice himself.

---

* This is especially the case when it comes to poverty and other deprivation. In their powerful book *Scarcity: The New Science of Having Less and How It Defines Our Lives*, Sendhil Mullainathan and Eldar Shafir show that being strapped for time or money or options imposes a huge demand on our mental bandwidth that can prevent us from making wise future-focused decisions.

"I'm very transparent about being forty-three and not having any money. I only wish more forty-three-year-olds had been honest with me [when I was younger]," he said. "I'm telling the cautionary tale of the grasshopper."

All deep structure regrets reveal a need and yield a lesson. With foundation regrets, the human need it lays bare is stability: we all require a basic infrastructure of educational, financial, and physical well-being that reduces psychological uncertainty and frees time and mental energy to pursue opportunity and meaning.

The lesson reaches back two and a half millennia. Think ahead. Do the work. Start now. Help yourself and others to become the ant.

"When I was 13 I quit the saxophone because I thought it was too uncool to keep playing. Ten years later I realize oh how wrong I was with that assessment."

Male, 23, California

//

"Thinking that working eighteen hours a day, six days a week, when I first started out would help me become successful. Instead, I destroyed my marriage and almost my health."

Male, 68, Virginia

//

"I regret not getting married in front of my mother. My husband-to-be was in the military and we had to get married fast and in Oklahoma, which is far from Ohio. She was very ill and died a month later. I could have given her the happiness of seeing me married and I selfishly didn't work to make that happen."

Female, 51, Ohio

8.

Boldness Regrets

One November evening in 1981, a twenty-two-year-old American named Bruce was on a train speeding northward through France when a young woman boarded at a Paris station and took the seat next to him. Bruce's French was meager. But the woman's English was decent, and they began talking.

Bruce had spent the past year in Europe. He'd lived with a family in Sweden, worked odd jobs, and hitchhiked across the continent. Now he was heading to Stockholm to catch a flight back to the United States. He was in a hurry; his Eurail pass expired the next day.

The woman, a brunette perhaps a year or two younger than he, was from Belgium. She'd been working in Paris as an au pair, and was traveling back to her small Belgian hometown for a short break.

The conversation came easily. Soon the two were laughing.

Then they were playing hangman and doing crossword puzzles. Before long, they were holding hands.

"It was truly as if we had known each other our whole lives," Bruce told me recently. "And I have never felt that way again."

The train chugged on. The hours raced by. Just before midnight, as the train was approaching a station in Belgium, the woman stood up and told him, "I have to go."

"I'll come with you!" Bruce said.

"Oh, God," she replied. "My father would kill me!"

They walked through the train aisle to the door. They kissed. Bruce madly scribbled his name and his parents' Texas address on a slip of paper and handed it to her. The train doors parted. She stepped off. The doors closed.

"And I just stood there stunned," said Bruce, who is now in his sixties and who asked that I not use his last name.

When he returned to his seat, his fellow passengers asked why he hadn't left the train with his girlfriend.

"We just met!" Bruce told them. He didn't even know her name. They hadn't exchanged names, Bruce explained, because "it was almost as if we already knew."

The following day, having made it to Stockholm, Bruce boarded a flight back to the United States.

Forty years later, when he completed the World Regret Survey, he relayed this tale and concluded, "I never saw her again, and I've always wished I stepped off that train."

I f foundation regrets arise from the failure to plan ahead, work hard, follow through, and build a stable platform for life, boldness regrets are their counterpart. They arise from the failure to take full advantage of that platform—to use it as a springboard into a richer life. Sometimes boldness regrets emerge from an accumulation of decisions and indecisions; other times they erupt from a single moment. But whatever their origin, the question they present us is always the same: Play it safe or take a chance?

With boldness regrets, we choose to play it safe. That may relieve us at first. The change we're contemplating may sound too big, too disruptive, too challenging—too hard. But eventually the choice distresses us with a counterfactual in which we were more daring and, consequently, more fulfilled.

Boldness regrets sound like this: *If only I'd taken that risk.*

SPEAKING UP AND SPEAKING OUT

Regrets of boldness often begin with a voice that isn't heard. Zach Hasselbarth, a thirty-two-year-old consumer lending manager in Connecticut, offered this to the World Regret Survey:

> I let the fear of what others would say stop me from being more outgoing in high school. I regret not taking more chances and being so shy.

"Back then," he told me in an interview, "I thought it was the end of the world if I got rejected; I thought it was the end of the world if they said no." So he lowered his head, never talked much, and rarely announced his presence. Later in life, thanks to a more fearless college roommate, Zach unlearned some of that behavior. But he still knocks himself for the opportunities he missed and the contributions he didn't make.

Several survey respondents used language almost identical to that of a thirty-five-year-old British Columbia man whose regret was "not learning to speak up for myself . . . in love, in school, in my family, or in my career." Some described "fearing my own voice." An enormous number of people of all ages and nationalities regretted being "too introverted."

Introversion and extroversion are fraught topics, in part because popular belief and legitimate science often depart. The conventional view, reinforced by the ubiquity of assessments like the Myers–Briggs Type Indicator, holds that we're either introverted or extroverted. But personality psychologists—the scientists who began studying the subject a hundred years ago—have long concluded that most people are a bit of both. Introversion and extroversion are not binary personality types. This trait is better understood as a spectrum—one where about two-thirds of the population lands in the middle.[1] Yet almost nobody in either the quantitative or qualitative regret surveys described excesses of extroversion, while many lamented tilting toward the other side of the scale.

For example, a California man regretted using his "introvert tendency as an excuse" for "not speaking up" in the classroom, the office, and even "when competing athletically."

A forty-eight-year-old woman in Virginia said:

I regret allowing my shyness [and] introversion . . . to keep me from moving to a larger market where job opportunities, activities, and dating pools are better than where I am living now.

A fifty-three-year-old man from the United Kingdom said:

I regret being too shy and polite as a teenager and young adult, always taking the safe path and not offending people. I could have taken more risks, been more assertive, and had more life experiences.

As a card-carrying ambivert who prefers the company of quiet people, I've cheered from the sidelines when others have decried the "extrovert ideal" in Western culture. Yet the evidence shows that modest efforts to move slightly in that direction can be helpful. For instance, Seth Margolis and Sonja Lyubomirsky of the University of California, Riverside, have found that asking people simply to act like an extrovert for one week appreciably increased their well-being.[2]

Similarly, many people who overcame their apprehensions and poured out even a small tincture of temerity reported being transformed—including this fifty-six-year-old North Carolina woman:

> I did not learn to find my own voice until having children and being their voice. Before that, particularly in school, I never said anything in classes where there were bullies or mean kids. I did not know how to speak up then. I wish I would not have been so quiet.

STEPPING UP AND STEPPING OUT

A few months after his encounter on the Eurail train, Bruce was living in College Station, Texas, when his mother forwarded him a letter bearing a French stamp and Paris postmark that had arrived at her home. Inside was a sheet of paper filled top to bottom with billowing handwriting.

The letter's English was imperfect, and perhaps consequently, its sentiment was slightly inscrutable. Bruce now knew the woman's name—Sandra—but not much else. "Maybe it's crazy, but when I think about you, I'm smiling," Sandra wrote. "I'm sure you understand what I feel about although you don't know me well." The words sounded tender—except for the oddly perfunctory conclusion: "Have a great day!" Sandra didn't sign her last name, nor did she include a return address.

In the pre-internet era of the early 1980s, that halted communication. For Bruce, the doors had opened—and closed—again.

Rather than try to track her down, he chose to throw away the letter.

"I decided I could not keep it," he told me, "because I would dwell on it."

The pain of boldness regrets is the pain of "What if?" Thomas Gilovich, Victoria Medvec, and other researchers have repeatedly found that people regret inactions more than actions—especially in the long term. "Regrettable failures to act . . . have a longer half-life than regrettable actions," Gilovich and Medvec wrote in one of their early studies.[3] In my own American Regret Project survey, inaction regrets outnumbered action regrets by nearly two to one. And other research has likewise found a preponderance of inaction regrets even in less individualistic cultures, like those of China, Japan, and Russia.[4]

A key reason for this discrepancy is that when we act, we know what happened next. We see the outcome and that can shrink regret's half-life. But when we don't act—when we don't step off that metaphorical train—we can only speculate how events would have unfolded. "Because regrettable inactions are more alive, current, and incomplete than are regrettable actions, we are reminded of them more often," say Gilovich and Medvec.[5] Or as the American poet Ogden Nash once wrote in a long verse about the differences between regrets of commission and regrets of omission:

> It is the sin of omission, the second kind of sin,
> That lays eggs under your skin.[6]

The consequences of actions are specific, concrete, and limited. The consequences of inaction are general, abstract, and unbounded. Inactions, by laying eggs under our skin, incubate endless speculation.

That might be why boldness regrets in the realm of romance were pervasive. I could probably create my own Tinder-for-regrets smartphone app, given the hundreds of entries like that of a thirty-seven-year-old male in Ireland:

> Met the most amazing woman in college and never found the courage to ask her out.

Or the sixty-one-year-old woman from Oklahoma whose regret was:

> Not calling someone I've been in love with for forty-five years.

Or this, from a sixty-five-year-old California man who regretted:

> That I didn't ask her out. It would have been life changing.

Boldness regrets endure because the counterfactual possibilities are so vast. What if Bruce had left that train with Sandra that November evening? Perhaps just a short-lived December romance. Or maybe an adulthood spent in Europe rather than in the Pacific

Northwest, where he ended up. Or even a brood of Belgian-American children tired of hearing the sappy story of their parents' chance meeting.

At the heart of all boldness regrets is the thwarted possibility of growth. The failure to become the person—happier, braver, more evolved—one could have been. The failure to accomplish a few important goals within the limited span of a single life.

The world of work, which most of us inhabit for more than half our waking hours, was especially fertile soil for these types of regrets. One thirty-three-year-old South African woman spoke for many when she wrote:

> I regret not having the courage to be more bold earlier in
> my career and caring too much what other people thought of me.

Zach Hasselbarth, one of the people who regretted early shyness, recalls growing up in Albany, the capital of New York. "In Albany, you get a job. You go to work for New York State. You retire in twenty years. You have a pension, and then you die," he told me. It was always easy to retreat into comfort, harder to pedal into uncertainty. Zach's own father didn't take many chances. But he told his son to abide what he said and not what he did. And what Zach's father said was, "Don't play it safe."

Many of those who did play it safe in their careers look at their choices from the vantage of midlife and wish they hadn't. A fifty-six-year-old man in Pennsylvania regrets "staying with my current company when I knew over fourteen years ago it would never satisfy," just as a fifty-three-year-old man from Great Britain regrets "not leaving my safe job to follow my instinct and stay true to my core values sooner." A fifty-four-year-old woman in Oregon regrets "not being bolder in my late thirties and taking a job in a new geographical area." Then she collapses her regret to a single word: "Settling."

One especially common boldness regret was not starting a business of one's own. After years of working for a large pharmaceutical company, Nicole Serena did create a business, a consultancy and training company near Toronto. Her regret: not doing it sooner.

"I should have taken bolder actions earlier in my career," said one California entrepreneur. "I got there eventually but wasted time listening to authority."

A few respondents who launched businesses that closed down expressed regrets about excessive risk. They failed, they said, because they weren't savvy or skilled enough or because they didn't appreciate the demands of entrepreneurship. But these people represented a distinct minority compared with those who regretted never taking the leap. Many even hoped for a second try. For example, in 1997, the early days of the internet, Doug Launders started a web training company in central Florida. The venture "survived a few years and then failed," he said.

> I fell off the horse and decided that riding horses wasn't for me. I spent the next twenty years handling the plow behind other people's horses. I regret never getting back on the horse. At fifty-seven, I'm still trying to figure out how.

For some people, unrealized growth from their failure to take a risk was professional. But for many, it was personal. Many boldness regrets reflect a desire to grow not for any instrumental reasons but because of the inherent value of growth itself. For example, hundreds of people in the survey who turned down earlier opportunities to travel listed that decision as their top regret. If my regret-based dating app fails, I could instead launch an

Expedia-for-the-regretful site, which would include special travel packages for the legions of college graduates in the surveys who regretted not studying abroad.

"It's not the bad or stupid things I've done but the things I didn't do that have caused me the most regret in life," said Gemma West of Adelaide, Australia.

[My] biggest regret is not going backpacking around Europe when I was eighteen, because I was scared—an important rite of passage for Australians and something my best friend did with someone else.

A forty-seven-year-old woman from Utah said:

I regret not traveling more when I was younger—before I had a mortgage and child and "real job" and all the responsibilities of being an adult. Because now, I don't feel like I have the freedom to do it.

Said a forty-eight-year-old Ohio man:

I regret not being more adventurous . . . taking time to travel, explore, and experience more of what the world has to offer. I let the fear of disappointment rule me and allowed others' expectations to be more important than my own. I was always the "good soldier" and worked hard to please those around me. I have a good life—I just wish I had more experiences to share with others. Someday . . .

Boldness regrets, as with the Ohio man above, are often about exploration. And some of the most significant exploration, respondents said, is inward. Authenticity requires boldness. And when authenticity is thwarted, so is growth. The most telling demonstration of this point came from several dozen people from all over the world who described their regret—their failure to be bold—with the same five words: "Not being true to myself."

People who asserted their identities rarely regretted it, even when those identities ran counter to the dominant culture. People who suppressed their identities talked about denying themselves the potential to live fully.

Take this fifty-three-year-old Californian:

> I regret not coming out as a gay man sooner. It definitely impacted how I showed up and my performance and connectedness with my colleagues.

Or a fifty-year-old Massachusetts woman:

> As a minority woman and immigrant, I regret not speaking up or educating when others ridiculed me because of my accent, skin color, and culture.

Or this submission, from a thirty-six-year-old New Yorker:

> I regret not coming out as a lesbian to my parents early in life. I spent a lot of years pretending I'm straight, and [have] never been able to tell the world that I love a woman.

Sometimes the ultimate act of boldness involves the risk of using one's voice in ways that might rattle others but that clear a new path for oneself.

TRAINS, PLANES, AND SELF-ACTUALIZATION

Bruce never threw out Sandra's letter. He intended to. He even thought he had. But after one of our conversations, he began digging through old boxes and discovered it among a pile of papers. He hadn't seen it in forty years. "Sandra's handwriting resonated in my memory," he told me. Her loopy letters "looked familiar from the word games we played on paper." He even scanned the letter and emailed me a copy.

But he didn't show it to his wife. Bruce has been married since the mid-1980s, and has two adult children. But he's never told his wife the story of the train or mentioned either the woman or the letter. It's not that he believes she would consider it a betrayal. It's more because of what such a conversation might expose.

"I wouldn't bring myself to say I regret my marriage, but it's also been a very difficult one," he said. "There are lots of reasons for staying married. And part of it is that you say you will."

"Do you ever think about what would have happened if you had gotten out at that stop in Belgium?" I asked him.

"I have. But I also don't let myself think about it too much because that will create a new regret. I don't want the regret to be the foundation for a gigantic infrastructure of regret!" he joked.

Yet after reading the letter again, he posted a message in the "missed connections" section of Craigslist Paris in the slim hope of locating Sandra. It's a lone flare sent into forty years of darkness—a flailing and perhaps final attempt to answer "What if?"

Should he find her—with the two once-young passengers now in their sixties—Bruce wouldn't make the same mistake again. He'd seize the chance to spend time with her, no matter what came of it.

All deep structure regrets reveal a need and yield a lesson.

With boldness regrets, the human need is growth—to expand as a person, to enjoy the richness of the world, to experience more than an ordinary life.

The lesson is plain: Speak up. Ask him out. Take that trip. Start that business. Step off the train.

"I regret not fighting this kid Ray in the summer of 1991. I walked away and always regretted not standing up for myself."

Male, 44, Nebraska

//

"I regret having an abortion. I was young, in college, and scared, but it has haunted me ever since."

Female, 34, Indiana

//

"Taking so long to come out as lesbian."

Female, 32, Brazil

9.

Moral Regrets

Kaylyn Viggiano had been married only a year when a man who'd recently befriended her and her husband, Steven, stopped by their apartment unexpectedly. Kaylyn was twenty-one at the time. She and Steven had met in high school, and they'd grown up near each other on the outskirts of Chicago amid a tight cluster of friends and extended family. Now they were living deep in Southern California, two hours from the Arizona border, where Steven, a U.S. Marine, was stationed. Life wasn't easy. Kaylyn had left nursing school when Steven started boot camp, and she followed him first to Virginia and next to this dry patch of desert where she knew almost nobody.

The friend, another Marine, had arrived when he knew Steven would not be home. He told Kaylyn—falsely—that Steven had been informing his colleagues that he no longer loved Kaylyn and was planning to leave her. Kaylyn—young, lonely, vulnerable—believed him. They had a few drinks, then a few more. And that led to Kaylyn's entry in the World Regret Survey two years later:

> I regret being unfaithful to my husband. That moment of weakness is not worth the pain that follows.

Joel Klemick had been married eleven years when, one October night, his wife, Krista, received an anonymous phone call. Joel, then thirty-five, and Krista, then thirty-two, were living in a mid-size city in central Canada where both had been raised and where they were raising their three children. After high school, Joel worked as a floor installer, but his professional trajectory changed early in his marriage after the couple discovered their local Christian and Missionary Alliance Church. Joel had entered seminary and was studying for a divinity degree. He was also working on the church staff as an associate pastor.

The caller that evening told Krista—accurately—that Joel had been seeing another woman. Krista confronted Joel with the accusation. He denied it. She pressed. He denied it again. She pressed again. He confessed. Krista asked him to leave their home. The church soon learned of Joel's transgression, and the board of directors fired him. Here's how Joel described his greatest regret:

> I began an extramarital affair that cost me my integrity, job, and friendships and almost cost me my family, a master's degree, and my faith.

M oral regrets make up the smallest of the four categories in the deep structure of regret, representing only about 10 percent of the total regrets. But for many of us, these regrets ache the most and last the longest. They are also more complex than the other core regrets. Nearly everyone agrees that constructing a strong life foundation—working hard in school, for example, or saving money—is wise. Many of us agree on what constitutes "boldness"—launching a business instead of settling into a lackluster job, traveling the world instead of lazing on the couch. But you and I and our nearly eight billion fellow humans don't share a single definition of what it means to be "moral."

The result is that moral regrets share a basic structure with their counterparts: they begin at the juncture of two paths. But they involve a wider set of values. For instance, we may find ourselves with a choice to treat someone with care or to harm them. Or maybe the choice is to follow the rules or to ignore them. Sometimes, we're faced with the option of remaining loyal to a group or betraying it; of respecting certain people or institutions or disobeying them; of preserving the sacred or desecrating it.

But whatever the specifics, at the pivotal moment, we choose what our conscience says is the wrong path. We hurt others. We hoodwink, connive, or violate the basic tenets of fairness. We break our vows. We disrespect authority. We degrade what ought to be revered. And while the decision can feel fine—even exhilarating— at first, over time it gnaws at us.

Moral regrets sound like this: *If only I'd done the right thing.*

THE MEANING OF MORALITY

Every so often you read a book that profoundly changes how you understand the world. For me, one of those books is *The Righteous Mind: Why Good People Are Divided by Politics and Religion*, written by Jonathan Haidt and published in 2012.[1] Haidt is a social psychologist, now at New York University, who devoted his early academic career to the study of moral psychology. In the book, he explains his and others' research about how people determine which actions are right and which are wrong.

The Righteous Mind led me to the underlying studies that Haidt wrote about, and they overturned my thinking on two key dimensions.

First, I'd long believed that when we face morally weighty questions (Is the death penalty justified? Should assisted suicide be legal?), we reason through the issues to arrive at a conclusion. We approach these questions like a judge who evaluates competing arguments, ponders both sides, and delivers a reasoned decision. But according to Haidt's research, that simply isn't accurate. Instead, when we consider what's moral, we have an instantaneous, visceral, emotional response about right or wrong—and then we use reason to justify that intuition.[2] The rational mind isn't a black-robed jurist rendering unbiased pronouncements, as I'd thought. It's the press secretary for our intuitions. Its job is to defend the boss.

The second dimension on which the book reshaped my perspective is especially relevant to this book. Morality, Haidt shows, is much broader and more varied than many secular, left-of-center Westerners typically understand. Suppose I asked—as Haidt, University of Southern California's Jesse Graham, and University of Virginia's Brian Nosek did in one paper[3]—whether it's wrong to "stick a pin into the palm of a child you don't know." All of us—liberal, conservative, middle-of-the-road—would say that it is. How could anyone endorse harming an innocent child? Likewise, if I asked about the morality of stealing money from a cash register when the clerk isn't looking, nearly everyone would agree that this, too, is wrong. When it comes to harming others for no reason or lying, cheating, and stealing, people of all backgrounds and beliefs generally concur on what's moral.

But for many political conservatives, not to mention many people outside North America and Europe, morality goes beyond the virtues of care and fairness. For example, is it wrong for children to talk back to their parents? To call adults by their first name? Is it wrong for an American to renounce his citizenship and defect to Cuba? Is it wrong to toss the Bible or the Koran into the garbage? Is it wrong for a woman to get an abortion, for a man to marry another man, or for people of any gender to wed multiple spouses? You will get different answers to these questions at a Baptist church and at a Unitarian church—in Blount County, Alabama, and in Berkeley, California. That's not because one group is virtuous and the other evil. It's because one group has a narrower view of morality (don't harm or cheat other people) and the other has a wider view (don't harm or cheat other people—but also stay loyal to your group, heed authority, and uphold the sacred).

Haidt and his colleagues call this idea "moral foundations theory."[4] Drawing on evolutionary biology, cultural psychology, and several other fields, they show that beliefs about morality stand on five pillars:

- **Care/harm:** Children are more vulnerable than the offspring of other animals, so humans devote considerable time and effort to protecting them. As a result, evolution has instilled in us the ethic of care. Those who nurture and defend the vulnerable are kind; those who hurt them are cruel.

- **Fairness/cheating:** Our success as a species has always hinged on cooperation, including exchanges that evolutionary scientists call "reciprocal altruism." That means we value those whom we can trust and disdain those who breach our trust.

- **Loyalty/disloyalty:** Our survival depends not only on our individual actions, but also on the cohesiveness of our group. That's why being true to your team, sect, or nation is respected—and forsaking your tribe is usually reviled.

- **Authority/subversion:** Among primates, hierarchies nourish members and protect them from aggressors. Those who undermine the hierarchy can place everyone in the group at risk. When this evolutionary impulse extends to human morality, traits like deference and obedience toward those at the top become virtues.[5]

- **Purity/desecration:** Our ancestors had to contend with all manner of pathogens—from *Mycobacterium tuberculosis* to *Mycobacterium leprae*—so their descendants developed the capacity to avoid them along with what's known as a "behavioral immune system" to guard against a broader set of impurities such as violations of chastity. In the moral realm, write one set of scholars, "purity concerns uniquely predict (beyond other foundations and demographics such as political ideology) culture-war attitudes about gay marriage, euthanasia, abortion, and pornography."[6]

Moral foundations theory doesn't say that care is more important than purity or that authority is more important than fairness or that you should follow one set of foundations instead of another. It simply catalogs how humans assess the morality of behavior. The theory is descriptive, not prescriptive. But its descriptive power is considerable. Not only did it reshape my understanding of both human reasoning and modern politics; it also offered an elegant way to interpret our moral regrets.

THE FIVE REGRETTED SINS

Deceit. Infidelity. Theft. Betrayal. Sacrilege. Sometimes the moral regrets people submitted to the surveys read like the production notes for a Ten Commandments training video. But the wide variety of regrets people reported sharpens into focus when viewed through the five moral frames I just described on the previous page. Two of the frames encompassed most of the regrets, but two of the other three were also well represented.

1. Harm

In the 1920s, when sociologists Robert Lynd and Helen Lynd began a long-term project to discover the soul of middle-class America for their classic book *Middletown*, the place where they chose to embed was Muncie, Indiana.[7] It was—and, in some ways, still is—the quintessential American small town. And it's where Steve Robinson had what is often the quintessential American childhood experience: bullying.

Steve moved to the Muncie area in eighth grade. He was a small kid, introverted and socially awkward. But he compensated

119

for these perceived deficits by becoming a menace. He taunted and teased his classmates. He picked fights. At age sixteen, he punched a fellow student and broke his two front teeth.

Now, at age forty-three, these gratuitous aggressions are Steve's deepest regrets.

People of all political persuasions agree: hurting someone who's not provoking us is wrong. No surprise, then, that in both the American Regret Project and the World Regret Survey, people reported more harm-related moral regrets than any other kind. And the most common harm was bullying. Even decades later, hundreds of respondents deeply regretted mistreating their peers.

For example, a fifty-two-year-old New York man admitted:

> I bullied a new kid in the seventh grade. He was from Vietnam and hardly spoke any English. Horrible!

A forty-three-year-old woman in Tennessee said:

> I made fun of a kid in middle school, dubbing him "Ziggy" for having a short, stubby body and spiky blond hair. I'll never forget the look on his face as he realized that the name would stick. It was cruel, putting me in the "power" position after I had endured years of bullying myself, but I regretted it immediately and have never done anything like it again.

Steve told me that in the moments preceding the bullying, "I knew I shouldn't be doing this." Yet he did. He enjoyed the attention. He relished the feeling of power. But he knew better. In fact, he'd occasionally been bullied himself, both at home and at school. "Having been on both sides of it, and knowing what it felt like, and then still having done it to someone else, is what I find most regretful," he told me.

Unlike boldness regrets, moral regrets are more likely to involve actions than inactions. But for some people, including Kim Carrington, simply being a bystander to bullying was enough to trigger regret.

When she was eight years old, Kim took a daily school bus from her small town on Minnesota's Iron Range to a larger town where her elementary school was located. Each day, the bus would pick up another girl, who lived in a farmhouse in a more remote area. And each day, when the girl boarded the bus, the other children would hold their noses as if she smelled, pelt her with rude names, and refuse to give her a place to sit.

One day, Kim scooted over in her seat to make room for the bullied girl. The two chatted amiably the rest of the ride. But because of that kindness, Kim herself was bullied at school that day. So, the following day, when the girl boarded, Kim refused to let the girl sit with her.

"I lost my integrity and it haunts me in the middle of the night and still makes me cry," said Kim, who is fifty and now lives in Kansas City. The other girl soon stopped riding the bus. "My regret is that I didn't befriend her. I didn't stand up for her. I did the wrong thing and never had a chance to make it better."

Regrets in this subcategory weren't limited to childhood malice. People described insulting work colleagues, "ghosting" romantic interests, and threatening neighbors. Most hurts were delivered with words, though a few were with fists. And for all the American associations of behavior like bullying, these regrets were international.

A fifty-three-year-old man from the United Kingdom:

I physically hurt a man when I was eighteen years old. I have spent the next thirty-five years hiding from life in every way. I am a coward.

A fifty-seven-year-old man from South Africa:

I regret telling a woman I was dumping her because she was fat. Thirty years later I'm waking up at night in disbelief at the hurt I caused then.

Hurting others is so unequivocally wrong that many people seek to channel the regret into more respectable future behavior. "You look back on your previous self and you're just embarrassed," Steve told me. But "as an adult, I've tried to be a better person." After graduating from high school, he earned degrees in psychology, nursing, and criminal justice. He's worked as a pediatric nurse and as a counselor to delinquent children. "I've done badly by people in the past and I want to do right by people in my current state," he told me. "There's a certain part of me that takes a lot of pride in trying to make people feel safe these days."

2. Cheating

Kaylyn and Joel, whose stories opened this chapter, weren't the only unfaithful spouses the World Regret Survey turned up. Regrets about hurting others, especially through bullying, were the most pervasive. But regrets about cheating, especially in marriages, finished a close second. On this, too, most people in most cultures agree: we should tell the truth, keep our promises, and play by the agreed-upon rules.

In a few instances, people confessed to cheating others out of physical items—from a sixteen-year-old in California who regretted "stealing cash from a box" to a fifty-one-year-old in Romania who wrote, "I am ashamed that I stole a harmonica from one of my army comrades."

Regrets about academic dishonesty, though not widespread, also spanned a range of ages—from a twenty-two-year-old woman in Virginia who wrote, "I regret cheating in school," to a sixty-eight-year-old man in New Jersey who wrote, "I regret having helped someone cheat on a calculus test . . . my freshman year. I have not figured out how to make that right."

But marital infidelity topped the list—with these regrets coming in from six continents and dozens of countries.

A fifty-year-old woman:

> I had an affair—worst mistake of my life. Now I always have to live with how awful I was to my husband. Instead of just being real and telling him how unhappy I was, I decided to do something so incredibly stupid that I'm not sure I can ever forgive myself.

And a fifty-year-old man:

> I regret the fact that I lost faith and strength in myself and cheated on my wife. I feel the regret every day.

A fifty-five-year-old woman:

> I cheated on my husband. He was an incredibly lovely man who loved his family. I am not even certain why I did this. I

loved him. I was a young mom of four children. We were a close family—we had fun, spent time together, really had no worries, and yet I still did that.

Harm and cheating overlap. Infidelity hurts the betrayed spouse. But what respondents seemed to regret the most, beyond the pain they inflicted, is the trust they shattered. "We took vows. I did betray him," Kaylyn told me. "I made vows to my wife that I destroyed," Joel said. "My integrity was out the window."

Jocelyn Upshaw, who works at the University of Texas (and who asked that I use a pseudonym instead of her real name), had a nine-month affair with a coworker at a moment when her marriage felt lifeless. She eventually told her husband. They went to therapy. The marriage survived. But the breach still nags at her.

"My husband and I made this commitment to each other. And I didn't keep my end of the bargain. My husband put his trust in me and I let him down," she told me. "Lying and cheating are pretty high on the 'don't do that' list if you're going to be a good person."

In the wake of their actions, Kaylyn, Joel, and Jocelyn worked to make things, if not right, at least better. Kaylyn confessed to her husband the morning after her indiscretion. "I've never been able to steal anything in my life. I've never cheated on a test. So, when this happened, I couldn't keep it in," she told me. Her husband stayed calm, and together they rebuilt trust. "He's the best man in the world," Kaylyn says.

Joel's passage was rockier. He subsequently fathered a child with the other woman. But he says he could never shake "the weight of accountability to a God who says, 'Do not commit adultery.'" He and his wife reconciled. They moved and began working at a church elsewhere in Canada. "To know that I betrayed my wife is one of the worst things to have to say," he told me. "My understanding of trust and trustworthiness has deepened, because I've experienced what it is to be untrustworthy."

Jocelyn, who is not religious, says her regret has made her more empathetic. "Before this happened, I had this sort of righteousness about me. I was the good kid. I would never do wrong. And then I did *really* wrong. That opened my eyes that people make mistakes." When she was younger, she says, she divided the world into good people and bad people. "It's taken me a long time to realize that's not true."

3. Disloyalty

When Charlie McCullough graduated from the University of Maryland in 1981 with a degree in mechanical engineering, he considered enlisting in the armed forces. He admired the dedication the military required and the camaraderie it fostered. But more lucrative job offers beckoned—and he chose the private sector. "Those who serve, especially in the military, really do love our country," he told me. "I regret I wasn't part of that."

Loyalty to a group is a core moral value. It's expressed with greater gusto in some political and national cultures than in others. And perhaps because of that, regrets about this moral foundation were not as numerous as those about harm and cheating.

What's more, the regrets people expressed were less about renouncing the group than falling short of one's obligations to it. For instance, among respondents in the United States, which ended active conscription in 1973 and does not require national service from its citizens, a large number of people offered reflections similar to Charlie's.

A forty-four-year-old woman in Michigan reported that her greatest regret was:

> Not joining the military and going into the air force.

A fifty-eight-year-old New Hampshire man regretted:

> I did not serve my country by joining the military prior to college or after college. Am the only member of my family not to join, and looking back, wish I had served.

A fifty-three-year-old woman in Wisconsin:

> I regret not joining a branch of the military. . . . Service to the country, no matter where or what the role, be it in Ameri-Corps, Peace Corps, etc., is tremendously valuable.

As Haidt writes in *The Righteous Mind*, the moral foundation of loyalty helps groups cement bonds and form coalitions. It shows "who is a team player and who is a traitor, particularly when your team is fighting with other teams."[8]

To my mild disappointment, the surveys unearthed not a single modern-day Benedict Arnold or Judas Iscariot. Charlie, in fact, ended up working for a large defense contractor that equips the armed forces. Yet merely being adjacent to the military was insufficient. He regrets not having "the experience of hardship and sacrifice," of depending on others for survival and of their relying on him. "If you're serving someone, it means you're not serving yourself," he told me. "The act of sacrifice is good for the other, but it's also good for the soul."

4. Subversion

The fewest moral regrets involved the Authority/Subversion foundation. A handful of people regretted "dishonoring my parents" and "being disrespectful to my teachers"—like the twenty-four-year-old man from India, who relayed this tale:

> My father and I run a shop. A teacher who taught me at school comes for shopping. My teacher knows me and my father, but my father doesn't know him. We give a little discount to whoever who has a long relationship with us and my teacher is among them. I thought my father knew him, so I didn't tell him that he was my teacher. Sir paid full amount, not that he minded. But after he left, my father demanded that I should have told him that he was sir. It was such a shame and disrespectful for us that we didn't discount the price to show some respect and gratitude. I deeply, deeply regret that incident every time that memory is recalled.

Such entries, though, were relatively rare. One reason for the dearth of this type of moral regret is that the quantitative portion of my survey sampled only Americans and the qualitative portion included more respondents from the United States than from any other country. Had I taken larger samplings in nations and regions where the cultural values of deference are often more prominent, this type of regret might have been more common.

5. Desecration

Regrets about violating sanctity were more numerous than regrets about subverting authority. These regrets were also emotionally intense—especially when they centered on one of the most fiercely contested issues of the last sixty years: abortion.

Americans share a rough consensus about abortion's legality, but they are deeply split on its morality. According to Gallup, about three-quarters of people in the United States believe that abortion should be legal in at least certain circumstances. However, 47 percent believe it is "morally wrong," while 44 percent believe it is "morally acceptable."[9] That divide came out clearly in my research.

Regrets about abortions were not as pervasive as regrets about bullying and infidelity, but they were prevalent. A fifty-year-old woman in Arkansas said:

> I had an abortion at age twenty. That is the biggest regret of my life. My second-biggest regret is that I had another one at age twenty-five.

These regrets were partly about harm, but they were bigger than that: a belief that the actions amounted to a degradation of the very sanctity of life.

For example, a sixty-year-old woman from Pennsylvania wrote:

> I regret that I aborted a fetus that would have been my third child with my husband. We've been married for thirty-four years. I had a tough pregnancy with my second. My husband did not want me to go through the suffering of another pregnancy just less than a year after our second child was born. I believe his thoughts were [also] the financial burden of a third child. . . . I cried the whole way to the clinic and have grieved every day since. . . . The burden of ending a life, a life created with love, bears on me every moment of every day.

A fifty-eight-year-old woman in Puerto Rico regretted:

> Having an abortion. Having to say I'm sorry when I meet him/her in Heaven.

More than a hundred years ago, the French sociologist Émile Durkheim wrote that the defining feature of religious thought—and, I'd argue, many other belief systems—is "the division of the world into two domains, one containing all that is sacred and the other all that is profane."[10] We don't always agree on the boundaries between those domains. But when we forsake what we believe is sacred for what we believe is profane, regret is the consequence.

Moral regrets are a peculiar category. They are the smallest in number, yet the greatest in variety. They are the most individually painful. But they may also be the most collectively uplifting. There is something heartening about grown women and men waking up at night despairing over incidents decades earlier in their lives in which they hurt others, acted unfairly, or compromised the values of their community. It suggests that stamped somewhere in our DNA and buried deep in our souls is the desire to be good.

All deep structure regrets reveal a need and yield a lesson. With moral regrets, the need is goodness. The lesson, which we've heard in religious texts, philosophy tracts, and parental admonitions, is this: when in doubt, do the right thing.

喂养一只兔子, 因为溺宠, 放出铁笼子后, 吃多兔粮包装袋的塑料而去世.*

Female, 38, China

//

"Inaction. Not asking the girl out, not starting the business sooner, not applying to speak at the conference. I regret inaction more than any mistake I've ever made."

Male, 43, Canada

//

"Not taking my grandmother candy on her deathbed. She specifically requested it."

Male, 35, Arkansas

---

* "While feeding and petting a rabbit, I accidentally let him escape from his cage, and he then ate a bunch of plastic and died."

10.

Connection Regrets

To understand connection regrets, let me tell you the story of four women, two friendships, and a pair of doors.

The first woman is Cheryl Johnson, a native of Des Moines, Iowa, a resident of Minneapolis, Minnesota, and the former research director at a publishing company. Cheryl is in her early fifties. She's devoted to her husband, her gym, and her latest projects, a house she's building and a book she's writing.

In the late 1980s, Cheryl attended Drake University, also in Des Moines, where she became fast friends with the second woman in this tale. Her name is Jen.

Cheryl and Jen belonged to the same sorority and lived in a house with about forty other women.[1] Among the group, these two stood out for their seriousness and ambition. Cheryl became president of the sorority; Jen was elected president of the entire student body. "We took our college careers a little more seriously than the typical student, and that made us oddballs," Jen told me. "We connected in part because we felt on the fringes of things socially."

They talked all the time. They supported each other's enthusiasms and aspirations. They hatched big plans to take on the world.

Shortly after graduation in 1990, Jen married—Cheryl was a bridesmaid—and moved to Virginia. And shortly after that, Jen invited Cheryl to visit her at her new home. Jen said that she wanted Cheryl to meet a friend of Jen's husband, who she thought might be a good romantic match.

Cheryl was taken aback. She'd been dating another Drake student for two years. "I thought he was the one." Jen knew the guy, but Cheryl said, she "clearly did not think he was the one." Cheryl politely declined the invitation to visit. No drama. No hard feelings.

Over the next few years, Cheryl and Jen, living in different parts of the country at a time before widespread email, exchanged letters and cards. Cheryl eventually ditched the boyfriend, whom she refers to today only as "Mr. Wrong," and says, "Now that I've matured into the person I am, I can see what Jen saw."

Within a couple of years, the letters dwindled. Then they stopped. Cheryl hasn't talked to Jen for twenty-five years. They haven't seen each other in person since Jen's wedding.

"We didn't have a falling out of any kind. I just let it kind of drift away," Cheryl told me. "I regret not having that relationship in my life. I've missed having another person in my life who could share with me the kind of growth I've experienced over the years."

The absence disquiets her. "If you're going to die in a month, are there things you would want tied up?" Cheryl said. "I would like her to know that [the friendship] feels significant to me even twenty-five years later."

During a conversation over Zoom one spring afternoon, I asked Cheryl if she'd consider trying to revive the friendship—or at least to call, email, or write Jen.

"I think the door's open," she replied. "If I were not a coward, I would reach out."

Connection regrets are the largest category in the deep structure of human regret. They arise from relationships that have come undone or that remain incomplete. The types of relationships that produce these regrets vary. Spouses. Partners. Parents. Children. Siblings. Friends. Colleagues. The nature of the rupture also varies. Some relationships fray. Others rip. A few were inadequately stitched from the beginning.

But in every case, these regrets share a common plotline. A relationship that was once intact, or that ought to have been intact, no longer is. Sometimes, often because of a death, there is nothing more that we can do. However, many times, in many roles—daughter, uncle, sorority sister—we yearn to close the circle. But doing so requires effort, brings emotional uncertainty, and risks rejection. So we confront a choice: Try to make the relationship whole—or let it remain unresolved?

Connection regrets sound like this: *If only I'd reached out.*

CLOSED DOORS AND OPEN DOORS

The third woman in the story is Amy Knobler. Amy, who lives in Pasadena, California, grew up in Cherry Hill, New Jersey. In middle school, she met a girl whom I'll call Deepa.

Deepa was a latchkey kid whose parents worked demanding

jobs and whose house stood just blocks from the school they attended. Amy and Deepa would head there after classes, forging a friendship in the freedom of an empty house. Amy remembers those afternoons as some of the happiest times in her life. "It was everything you think about connecting with a close friend," she told me.

Amy and Deepa stayed friendly in high school, and stayed in touch after graduation as they moved on with college, careers, and families. Deepa came to Amy's wedding in 1998. Their families were so close that even Amy's parents attended Deepa's wedding in 2000. For a wedding gift, Amy gave Deepa an elaborate handmade cookbook of her favorite recipes. "There's no other connection like the kind you make in childhood, you know?" Amy said.

In 2005, Deepa's husband sent a note to all the people in his wife's life informing them that Deepa had been diagnosed with an aggressive form of cancer. As with many illnesses, the news that followed caromed between scary and reassuring. Deepa went into remission. She had a baby. But in the summer of 2008, the cancer returned and her prospects appeared grim. Deepa's quality of life was fine for the moment, the Facebook update notified friends and family, but she likely had only a year to live.

Amy wanted to call her old friend.

Amy put off calling her old friend.

Late one night in December of 2008, Amy received a message from a mutual friend that Deepa's health had taken a serious downward turn.

The following day, Amy called Deepa's home in New Jersey to speak with her. The person who answered the phone explained that Deepa had died earlier that morning.

"I will never forget how much I realized in that moment the opportunity that had been lost to me," Amy said. "My thought always was, 'Did she die wondering why I never called?' I will always wonder, and I just swore I was never going to behave that way again."

People often talk about regrets in terms of doors. Amy has a "closed door" regret. As she told me, the opportunity to restore her connection with Deepa is gone. Cheryl has an "open door" regret. The opportunity to reconnect with her college friend remains.

Both types of regrets nag at us, but for different reasons. Closed door regrets distress us because we can't do anything about them. Open door regrets bother us because we can, though it requires effort.

In the World Regret Survey, many participants reported the sense of loss that accompanies a door that has closed.

A fifty-one-year-old California man became disconnected from his father at age seven, when his parents divorced. He visited his father every other weekend, but "the relationship was shallow . . . no deep conversations, nor getting to really know each other." By middle school, the visits stopped. The man reconnected somewhat with his father in his late teens and early twenties, but:

> Still, during all that time we didn't get to build any sort of
> bond. . . . He passed away seventeen years ago, and I often regret
> not having a beer with him as adult men.

A fifty-four-year-old woman shared this:

> I regret not being nicer to my mom. I took her for granted
> when I was younger, thinking that I was so much smarter than
> she was (typical teenager). When I grew up, we argued over
> politics, both of us passionate about our viewpoints. Now that

she is gone, I miss her desperately, so much that it takes my breath away sometimes. I did the daughter thing all wrong. I look at my daughters and pray that they are kinder to me than I was to my own mom, even though I'm not sure I deserve it.

For many people, including a forty-five-year-old woman from the District of Columbia, the door closed with words left unspoken:

My brother died suddenly at forty-one. I regret not saying "I love you" more.

And several regrets resembled this one from a forty-four-year-old Iowa woman:

I regret not attending the funeral of my college coach and mentor. My baby was only a couple of weeks old, it was wintertime with a chance of bad weather, and it was over a three-hour drive. I type these excuses just as I told them to myself again and again in my decision-making process. I tried to convince myself I made the right decision. . . . Reason, regret, reason, regret, reason, regret play ping-pong in my brain whenever I think about that event from fifteen years ago.

A 2012 study by Mike Morrison, Kai Epstude, and Neal Roese concluded that regrets about social relationships are felt more deeply than other types of regrets because they threaten our sense of belonging. When our connections to others tatter or disintegrate, we suffer. And when it's our fault, we suffer even more. "The need to belong," they wrote, "is not just a fundamental human motive but a fundamental component of regret."[2]

Closed door regrets vex us, because we can't fix them. It's over. But doors that cannot budge hide behind them a benefit: they offer another example of how regret can make us better.

A few years after Deepa died, Amy learned that another childhood friend had been diagnosed with cancer. "I kept revisiting my previous experience [with Deepa]," Amy said. "I really needed to get myself on board for however difficult this would be."

Amy called this friend frequently. She visited her. They exchanged emails and texts. "I did as much as I was able to make sure she knew that she was always in my thoughts. I made a much more concerted effort to be present with her and acknowledge the reality of her situation."

The friend passed away in 2015. "We maintained a connection up until she died," Amy told me. "It didn't make it easier. But I don't have regrets."

RIFTS AND DRIFTS

Cheryl and Jen never argued—not even a small squabble. They never discussed the dissolution of their friendship. It simply faded.

While the connection regrets that people reported in the surveys numbered well into the thousands, the specific ways their relationships ended numbered only two: rifts and drifts.

Rifts usually begin with a catalyzing incident—an insult, a disclosure, a betrayal. That incident leads to raised voices, ominous threats, crashed plates, and other mainstays of telenovelas and Edward Albee plays. Rifts leave the parties resentful and antagonistic, even though to outsiders the underlying grievance might sound trivial and easy to repair.

For example, a seventy-one-year-old Canadian man regretted that:

A disagreement with my son at Christmas over the behavior of his five-year-old son (my grandson) turned into a huge, albeit brief, argument. It has resulted in a family estrangement that has lasted almost five years. We have not talked or communicated in any way since then.

A sixty-six-year-old Texas woman wrote:

I regret reacting negatively when I found out my daughter-in-law . . . and my son were immigrating back to her home in Australia after we were led to believe she wanted to live near us. They left and are now estranged.

Drifts follow a muddier narrative. They often lack a discernible beginning, middle, or end. They happen almost imperceptibly. One day, the connection exists. Another day, we look up, and it's gone. A Pennsylvania woman regretted:

Not taking time to be a better friend, sister, daughter. Letting time slip away and suddenly realizing that I'm forty-eight.

A forty-one-year-old man in Cambodia wrote:

I regret letting good friends drift away by not staying in touch.

For many, the situation is recognizable only in retrospect. Said a sixty-two-year-old Pennsylvania man:

I wish I had tried harder to foster deeper relationships with my work colleagues. I've worked at the same place for over thirty years, but I'm not sure I would really call any of the people I've worked with a close friend.

Rifts are more dramatic. But drifts are more common.

Drifts can also be harder to mend. Rifts generate emotions like anger and jealousy, which are familiar and easier to identify and comprehend. Drifts involve emotions that are subtler and that can feel less legitimate. And first among these emotions, described by hundreds of people with connection regrets, is awkwardness.

When Cheryl has contemplated reconnecting with her old friend, she's asked herself, "Would it be better for Jen not ever to hear from me—or for Jen to hear from me and have it be kind of creepy?" And Cheryl's concerns about creepiness have always prevailed. She worries about "the weirdness of reaching out" after a quarter century. She fears that such a gesture "might seem not right" to her friend.

The same barrier prevented Amy from telephoning Deepa. "There was a sort of awkwardness to me of 'I haven't really talked to you in years. But, hey, I heard you're dying and I'm going to call!'" Amy explained. "I wish I had not been afraid to confront the uncomfortable feelings I knew I was going to have when I called her."

If Amy had faced those feelings, she might have been surprised, even gratified. Human beings are impressive creatures. We can fly planes, compose operas, and bake scones. But we generally stink at divining what other people think and anticipating how they will behave. Worse, we don't realize how inept we are at these skills.[3] And when it comes to perceiving and predicting awkwardness, we're next-level bunglers.

In a 2014 study, social psychologists Nicholas Epley and Juliana Schroeder recruited commuters on trains and buses in the Chicago area and asked some of them to start conversations with strangers. The recruits predicted that doing so would make them feel uncomfortable and that the recipients of their entreaties would suffer even greater awkwardness. They were mistaken on both fronts. Those who initiated conversations found it easier to do than they expected. They enjoyed their commute more than control group participants, who remained to themselves. And the strangers with whom they spoke were not put off. They enjoyed the conversations just as much.

"People misunderstand the consequences of social connection," Epley and Schroeder wrote.[4] Commuters feared that reaching out would be uncomfortable for everyone, but their fears were misplaced. It wasn't awkward at all.

In a 2020 study, Erica Boothby of the University of Pennsylvania and Vanessa Bohns of Cornell University examined a related phenomenon: our squeamishness about complimenting other people. The prospect of giving compliments, Boothby and Bohns found, can make people skittish. They worry "their awkwardness is on display and that people are noticing—and judging—them for their many flaws and faux pas." But in the experiments, people's predictions—about themselves and others—proved way off. They drastically *overestimated* how "bothered, uncomfortable, and annoyed" the person receiving their compliment would feel—and *underestimated* how positively that person would react.[5] It wasn't awkward at all.

What's going on in these situations is a phenomenon that social psychologists call "pluralistic ignorance." We mistakenly assume that our beliefs differ vastly from everyone else's—especially when those private thoughts seem at odds with broader public behavior. So, when we struggle to understand a lecture, we don't ask questions because we erroneously believe that because other people aren't asking questions, that means *they* understand—and we don't want to look dumb. But we don't consider that other people might be equally befuddled—and equally nervous about seeming stupid. We're confused, but we stay confused because we falsely believe nobody but us is confused! Or surveys of college students reveal that most students don't drink excessively. But those students think that they're the exception, and that all their classmates are constantly getting hammered, which perversely reinforces a social norm that relatively few people truly endorse.[6]

Our concerns about the awkwardness of reconnecting with someone from whom we've drifted conform to this pattern. We too often presume that our own preferences are unique. During a conversation in which Cheryl maintained that Jen would have little interest in reconnecting—and that she would instead consider any communication from Cheryl a little creepy—I asked her to consider the reverse scenario.

How would she feel if Jen reached out to her?

"If I got a message from her today, oh my God, I would burst into tears," she told me. "That would be a life-changing thing for me to hear from her and for her to still be thinking about our friendship after all those years."

"HAPPINESS IS LOVE. FULL STOP."

The longest-running examination of the lifetime well-being of a single group of people is the Study of Adult Development at Harvard Medical School, also known as the Grant Study, for one of its creators. You might have heard of it. In 1938, researchers at Harvard recruited 268 undergraduate men, and followed them for the next eighty years. The length of the study and its detail are astounding. Researchers measured the men's IQ, analyzed their handwriting, and examined their brows and testicles. They drew blood, took electroencephalograms, and calculated their lifetime earnings. The audacious goal was to try to determine why some people flourished in work and life and others floundered.

Despite its obvious limitations—the subjects were all white American men—the Grant Study is one of the most important long-term projects in the history of psychological science. Researchers eventually included the offspring and spouses of these men in the study. And in the 1970s they added 456 working-class Bostonians to diversify the socioeconomic pool. The combined conclusions of these efforts are considered serious, instructive, and probably universal.

As the *Harvard Gazette* summarized in 2017:

> Close relationships, more than money or fame, are what keep people happy throughout their lives. . . . Those ties protect people from life's discontents, help to delay mental and physical decline, and are better predictors of long and happy lives than social class, IQ, or even genes. That finding proved true across the board among both the Harvard men and the inner-city participants.[7]

Men who'd had warm childhood relationships with their parents earned more as adults than men whose parent-child bonds were more strained. They were also happier and less likely to suffer dementia in old age. People with strong marriages suffered less physical pain and emotional distress over the course of their lives. Individuals' close friendships were more accurate predictors of healthy aging than their cholesterol levels. Social support and connections to a community helped insulate people against disease and depression. Meanwhile, loneliness and disconnection, in some cases, were fatal.

In 2017, Robert Waldinger, a psychiatrist and the current director of the study, described to a journalist the core insight of the research: "Taking care of your body is important, but tending to your relationships is a form of self-care too. That, I think, is the revelation."[8]

Many people in the World Regret Survey seem to have arrived at a conclusion similar to what the Grant Study found. Take, for example, this fifty-seven-year-old California woman:

> I regret that I didn't cuddle more with my stepdaughter when she was a child. I didn't want her to think I was trying to replace her mother, and didn't realize how much she needed to be mothered.

Or a sixty-two-year-old Ohio woman, who said:

> Both my parents, although a year apart, did their hospice at my home. I deeply regret not spending more time on their last days holding hands and speaking about the lovely moments they gave me. We weren't a family that hugged, cried, or kissed, and I didn't know I needed to do that—for them or for me.

Or this seventy-one-year-old Floridian:

> When my daughter came out as transgender at the age of fourteen, I did not understand and did not handle the situation

well. As a result, I inflicted incredible pain on my only child and the person I love most in this world. Things have changed since then and I am her number one supporter now, but I will never forgive myself for not being the parent I should have been when it mattered most.

One remarkable (non)finding in the World Regret Survey involved parents. Hundreds of people described regrets about marrying the wrong spouse or choosing a disappointing partner, but fewer than twenty respondents out of more than sixteen thousand regretted having children.[9] In some sense, both behavioral science and popular culture have focused too much attention on romance and not enough on other forms of family connection. In fact, in 2020, a group of more than forty international scholars, representing two dozen countries, examined data from twenty-seven societies around the world and concluded that while academic journals were packed with research on mate-seeking, people across the globe actually "prioritize goals related to familial bonds over mating goals."[10] Directing more research to long-term family relationships, which produce greater and more enduring well-being with fewer downsides than romantic entanglements, would expand our understanding.

George Vaillant, another Harvard psychiatrist, headed the Grant Study for more than thirty years. In an unpublished 2012 manuscript, he reflected on what he'd learned from the experience. After eight decades, hundreds of subjects, thousands of interviews, and millions of data points, he said he could summarize the conclusion of the longest-running examination of human flourishing in five words: "Happiness is love. Full stop."[11]

In the end, the problem we contend with as people is remarkably simple. What give our lives significance and satisfaction are meaningful relationships. But when those relationships come apart, whether by intent or inattention, what stands in the way of bringing them back together are feelings of awkwardness. We fear that we'll botch our efforts to reconnect, that we'll make our intended recipients even more uncomfortable. Yet these concerns are almost always misplaced. Sure, we'll get rebuffed sometimes. But more often—*much* more often, in fact—we overestimate how awkward we'll feel and underestimate how much others will welcome our overtures.

So, this simple problem has an even simpler solution. Shove aside the awkwardness.

When Amy Knobler considers her closed door regret, she wishes she could travel backward in time and whisper advice to her previous self. She'd assure young Amy "that even though it feels awkward, and it is super uncomfortable and scary, on the other side of it, you will be glad that you went through that experience, not only because you don't have those unanswered questions in your mind at that point, but also for what it does for the other person."

And when Cheryl Johnson gazes at the open door of her relationship with Jen, she has an instinct about her next move even if she won't—for now at least—act on it: "You're almost always better off to err on the side of showing up. And if it's awkward, then it's awkward and you'll live. It'll be fine. But if you don't show up, it's lost forever."

All deep structure regrets reveal a need and yield a lesson. With connection regrets, the human need is love. Not love only in the romantic sense—but a broader version of love that includes attachment, devotion, and community and that encompasses parents, children, siblings, and friends.

The lesson of closed doors is to do better next time. The lesson of open doors is to do something now. If a relationship you care about has come undone, place the call. Make that visit. Say what you feel. Push past the awkwardness and reach out.

"My biggest regrets stem from not being more assertive at various life points about my needs and wishes—education, relationships, vacation plans, right down to the food that winds up in my house."

Male, 51, New Jersey

//

"I wish I had planted more trees."

Male, 57, United Kingdom

//

"I regret putting my life on display for so long on social media. There are too many times I overshared and now it feels like too much of me is just 'out there.'"

Female, 27, Washington

Opportunity
and Obligation

Photography was more complicated and expensive back in the twentieth century before every phone had a camera and every pocket had a phone. Gather round, youngsters, and I'll explain.

In those bygone days, photographers shot their photos on film. They'd press a button to open their camera's shutter, which would momentarily let in light. The light would then interact with chemicals on the film to memorialize an image.

The result was a bit odd. On the strip of film that photographers removed from the camera, the light spots appeared dark and the dark spots light. This was called a "negative"—and it was the middle step in the production process. When photographers printed that negative on paper, the light and dark would be reversed and the original color tones restored.

Regret works much the same way. The four core regrets operate as a photographic negative of the good life. If we know what people *regret* the most, we can reverse that image to reveal what they *value* the most.

So, what do we all ultimately want and need?

The deep structure of regret, summarized in the table below, provides an answer.

THE DEEP STRUCTURE OF REGRET

	What it sounds like	The human need it reveals
Foundation	If only I'd done the work.	Stability
Boldness	If only I'd taken the risk.	Growth
Moral	If only I'd done the right thing.	Goodness
Connection	If only I'd reached out.	Love

We seek a measure of stability—a reasonably sturdy foundation of material, physical, and mental well-being.

We hope to use some of our limited time to explore and grow— by pursuing novelty and being bold.

We aspire to do the right thing—to be, and to be seen as, good people who honor our moral commitments.

We yearn to connect with others—to forge friendships and family relationships bonded by love.

A solid foundation. A little boldness. Basic morality. Meaningful connections. The negative emotion of regret reveals the positive path for living.

COULDA AND SHOULDA

Each time you look in the mirror, you see one person. But if you squint a little harder, you might see three *selves*.

That is the idea animating a theory of motivation that Tory Higgins, a Columbia University social psychologist, first proposed in 1987. Higgins argued that we all have an "actual self," an "ideal self," and an "ought self."

Our actual self is the bundle of attributes that we currently possess. Our ideal self is the self we believe we *could* be—our hopes, wishes, and dreams. And our ought self is the self we believe we *should* be—our duties, commitments, and responsibilities.[1]

What fuels our behavior and directs which goals we pursue, Higgins argued, are discrepancies between these three selves. For instance, if my ideal self is someone who's healthy and physically fit but my actual self is lethargic and overweight, that gap might motivate me to start exercising. If my ought self believes in caring for elderly relatives but my actual self hasn't visited Grandma in six months, I might leave the office early and to Grandmother's house I will go. However, when we don't make these efforts, when a discrepancy persists between who we are and who we could or should be, unpleasant feelings flood the gap.

In 2018, Shai Davidai, of the New School for Social Research, and the ubiquitous Thomas Gilovich enlisted Higgins's theory to analyze regret. Expanding on Gilovich's earlier research showing that, over time, people regret inactions more than actions, they conducted six studies that reached a single conclusion: people regret their failures to live up to their ideal selves more than their failures to live up to their ought selves. Regrets of "coulda" outnumbered regrets of "shoulda" by about three to one.

The likely reason is the contrasting emotional consequences of these two flavors of regret. Discrepancies between our actual self and our ideal self leave us dejected. But discrepancies between our actual self and our ought self make us *agitated*—and therefore more likely to act. We feel a greater sense of urgency about ought-related regrets, so we're more likely to begin repair work—by undoing past behavior, apologizing to those we've wronged, or learning from our mistakes.[2] "Couldas" bug us longer than "shouldas," because we end up fixing many of the "shouldas."*

This analysis offers another window into the deep structure of regret. Failures to become our ideal selves are failures to pursue *opportunities*. Failures to become our ought selves are failures to fulfill *obligations*. All four of the core regrets involve opportunity, obligation, or both.

For example, boldness regrets—*If only I'd taken that risk*—are entirely about opportunities we didn't seize.[3] Foundation regrets—*If only I'd done the work*—are also largely about opportunities (for education, health, financial well-being) that we didn't pursue. Connection regrets—*If only I'd reached out*—are a mix. They involve opportunities for friendship we didn't follow through on, as well as obligations to family members and others that we neglected. Moral regrets—*If only I'd done the right thing*—are about obligations we didn't meet.

The result is that opportunity and obligation sit at the center of regret, but opportunity has the more prominent seat. This also helps explain why we're more likely to regret what we didn't do than what we did. As Neal Roese and Amy Summerville have written, "Regrets of inaction last longer than regrets of action in part because they reflect greater perceived opportunity."[4]

The importance of opportunity became clearer when I reexamined the data I collected in the American Regret Project, the quantitative portion of my research. The size and breadth of this survey allowed me to investigate differences between subgroups.

---

* This idea also emerges in *The Top Five Regrets of the Dying: A Life Transformed by the Dearly Departing*, a 2012 book in which hospice nurse Bronnie Ware recorded the regrets of some of her patients. One prominent regret involved patients telling her, "I wish I'd had the courage to live a life true to myself, not the life others expected of me."

Do women's regrets differ from men's? Do Black Americans hold different regrets than White Americans? Do life regrets depend on whether you're rich or poor?

The short answer is that group differences were not massive. The longer and more intriguing answer is that the differences that did emerge reinforced the centrality of opportunity as a driver of regret.

Take, for example, the education level of respondents. People with college degrees were more likely to have career regrets than people without college degrees. At first that might seem surprising. Having a college degree generally affords people a wider set of professional options. But that could be precisely why college graduates have more career regrets. Their lives presented more opportunities—and therefore a larger universe of foregone opportunities.

Income presented a similar pattern. Regrets about finance, not surprisingly, correlated tightly with household income—the lower the household income, the more likely someone was to have a finance-related regret. But regrets about careers ran in the *reverse* direction. That is, the higher the income, the more likely it was that someone had a career regret. Again, more opportunities could beget more regrets about unrealized opportunities.

Regrets about education were most prevalent among people who had attended college but had not graduated. For one in four people in this group, education constituted their greatest regret. In this case, impeded opportunity may be the reason.

Thwarted opportunity is the likely reason for the one racial gap that emerged in the survey. Racial differences in regret were minimal—except on a single dimension. People who were not White had more regrets about education than White people, which is likely explained by the racial disparities in access to educational opportunities in the United States.

Age also showed the importance—and paradox—of opportunity.

In the American Regret Project survey, twenty-year-olds had equal numbers of action and inaction regrets. But as people grew older, inaction regrets began to dominate. By age fifty, inaction regrets were twice as common as action regrets. Indeed, according to the data, age was by far the strongest predictor of regrets of inaction. When the universe of opportunities before them has dwindled (as it has with older folks), people seem to regret what they haven't done.

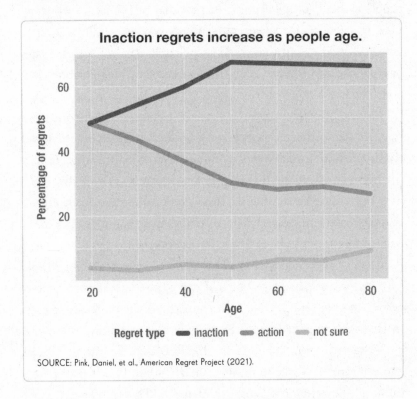

Inaction regrets increase as people age.

SOURCE: Pink, Daniel, et al., American Regret Project (2021).

Yet they also look for opportunities in different places. For example, among those ages thirty through sixty-five, regrets about career and finances were most prevalent—likely because, at that stage of life, opportunities were still alive in those realms. But as people aged, they tended to have fewer regrets about education, health, and career—and more regrets about family. One reason: at age seventy, the opportunities are relatively limited to get a PhD or launch a new career or compensate for decades of hard living. Those doors are closing. But the opportunity remains to reconcile with your estranged brother before both of you pass on. That door remains open.

Differences between men and women were not vast, but they were present. For example, men were more likely than women to have career regrets. About one in five men expressed regrets in this category, but only 12 percent of women. By contrast, women were more likely than men to have family regrets—24 percent of women versus 18 percent of men. The survey didn't ask questions that can deliver a definitive explanation for this difference. But we can speculate that men, on average, may be more likely to value professional opportunities, and women, on average, may be more likely to value relationship opportunities.*

DREAMS AND DUTIES

We regret foregone opportunities more often than unfulfilled obligations. Yet we also know that a wholly realized life involves a mix of both dreams and duties.[5] The photographic negative that

---

* One gender difference that comes out in the existing research involves sexual regrets. A 2013 study led by Andrew Galperin and Martie Haselton of UCLA found that in general, men's sexual regrets involve inactions—people they didn't sleep with. Women's sexual regrets more often involve actions—people they did sleep with. Likewise, Neal Roese has shown that men's romantic regrets typically involve inactions, while women's romantic regrets are more evenly split between actions and inactions. (See: Galperin, Andrew, Martie G. Haselton, David A. Frederick, Joshua Poore, William Hippel, David M. Buss, and Gian C. Gonzaga. "Sexual regret: Evidence for evolved sex differences." *Archives of Sexual Behavior* 7, no. 42 (2013): 1145–61; Roese, Neal J., Ginger L. Pennington, Jill Coleman, Maria Janicki, Norman P. Li, and Douglas T. Kenrick. "Sex differences in regret: All for love or some for lust?" *Personality and Social Psychology Bulletin* 32, no. 6 (2006): 770–80.)

regret offers makes clear that being fully human combines our dreams for ourselves and our duties to others.

A life of obligation and no opportunity is crimped. A life of opportunity and no obligation is hollow. A life that fuses opportunity and obligation is true.

How to build that life by transforming your existing regrets and anticipating your future regrets is the subject of the rest of this book.

Part Three

REGRET
REMADE

//

"I stopped being nice to Jessica, and when she got her period at school, which lasted three days, I called her Bloody Mary."

Female, 39, North Carolina

//

"I regret every kiss I could have given to my wife but didn't because I was too busy during our sixty-two years of marriage before she died of COVID."

Male, 84, Texas

//

"I regret not learning how to read music or play an instrument. I realize now it is a valuable skill that's good for you even if you are not into music."

Female, 17, Japan

12.

Undoing and
At Leasting

J eff Bosley was just trying to be cool.

He'd enlisted in the U.S. Army at age twenty-nine, and was now the oldest grunt at Fort Bragg—older even than his drill sergeant. He wanted to fit in. So, one night, he and a few buddies left the base, drove into town, and entered a tattoo shop.

Jeff was seeking an image or phrase that would impress his comrades, a "hyper-macho" symbol, as he put it, to broadcast his warrior philosophy. He chose his left arm as the tattoo's site, because "that's the arm I'd see when I'm holding my rifle barrel."

The shop artist opened a Microsoft Word program on a nearby computer, and they selected the Papyrus font. And there on Jeff's left arm, for about one hundred dollars, the artist inked nine black letters:

NO REGRETS

Jeff served in the army for nearly a decade and became a Green Beret. After the military, he worked as a firefighter in Colorado Springs, Colorado. During that stage of his life, he and his wife of twelve years divorced. And when his marriage ended, he discovered something about himself: *he had plenty of regrets.* He regretted not taking college—eight years, two schools, no degree—more seriously. He regretted hurting his wife by seeking a divorce. He regretted never pursuing his longtime love of acting.

Fourteen years after that impetuous evening decision, Jeff realized that his tattoo wasn't just unaesthetic. (The Papyrus font is "the lamest and most cliché I could have chosen," he told me.) It was also untrue.

"Regret is a thing," Jeff said when we talked. "I do have regret. It fuels me. Regret sucks, but I like that better than people who say, 'No regrets,' or, 'I don't have regrets.'"

Prodded by this regret, he moved from central Colorado to Southern California, where he's now making a living as an actor. And prodded by the constant reminder of a credo he no longer believed, he decided to have the NO REGRETS tattoo removed. The process is painful, time-consuming, and expensive. It involves regular laser sessions at a dermatology office and costs more than ten times the original ink.

"Every time I go to the removal place, if it's a new nurse or technician, I say, 'I get it.' The joke is not lost on me."

What do we do with our regrets? If regrets make us human, how do we enlist them to make us better, more satisfied people?

The starting point is to revisit one of the key distinctions in the architecture of regret: the difference between regrets of action and regrets of inaction—between regretting what we did and regretting what we didn't do. Action regrets are less prevalent. And in this short chapter, I'll explain how you can transform them to adjust the present. In the next chapter, I'll take on the more complex challenge of how you can transform both varieties of regret to improve your future.

For action regrets, your initial goal should be to change the immediate situation for the better. That's not always possible, but we have two ways to advance toward that goal. We can undo many such regrets: we can make amends, reverse our choices, or erase the consequences. Think of Jeff and his now fading tattoo. We can also respond to action regrets by using *At Leasts* to help us feel better about our circumstances. Neither tack does much to prepare us for later, but both can help us realign now.

STEP 1. UNDO IT

Suppose that without provocation, you slapped your best friend in the face or said something snarky about the deceased to his relatives at his funeral. You'd probably regret it. Most of us would. But only an entertainment executive would see within these indiscretions the seeds of a television show.

Het Spijt Me was a program that began airing on Dutch television in 1993 and continued to run in various iterations for the next twenty years. The basic format of the show (in English, the title is *I Am Sorry*) always involved two protagonists. The first was the person with a regret—say, the one who'd smacked her bestie. The second was the person who'd been wronged—the individual on the receiving end of said smack.

In the original version of the show, the regretter, sitting on a couch, talk-show-style, before a studio audience, would tell *Het Spijt Me*'s host about her regret. Then together they'd watch footage of the show's producers tracking down the regrettee, hearing the story from her point of view, and asking if she'd accept an apology. It being Holland, flowers were always involved.

If the regrettee accepted the apology, she'd stride through a pair of sliding doors and greet the regretter on stage. (In subsequent versions of the program, the regretter waited down the street from the regrettee's home.) As amends were made, tears were shed and hugs exchanged.

Three Dutch researchers, led by social psychologist Marcel Zeelenberg, a leading scholar of regret, analyzed two seasons of *Het Spijt Me* to determine which regrets people sought to reverse. They found that on the show, as well as in the nontelevised parts of life, people are much more likely to undo regrets of action than regrets of inaction.[1] We're more apt to repair what we did than what we didn't do.

The reasons are many. As we saw in Chapters 8 and 9, action regrets typically arise from concrete incidents and elicit "hot" emotions that we respond to quickly. Inaction regrets, by contrast, are often more abstract and elicit less immediately intense emotions.

What's more, many inaction regrets are inherently difficult to undo. If in my twenties I regret not studying hard enough in high school, I can't reenroll in eleventh grade. My only option is to focus on the future.

But with regrets of action, I still have the chance to recalibrate the present—to press Ctrl+Z on my existential keyboard.* For instance, with moral regrets, which often involve actions like

---

* Since I'm a Mac user, in typing and in living, I can also press Command+Z.

bullying a weaker kid, cheating on a spouse, or insulting coworkers, one form of undoing is to apologize. Apologies, wrote the great sociologist Erving Goffman, are "admissions of blameworthiness and regret for an undesirable event that allow actors to try to obtain a pardon from audiences."[2] If that pardon is granted, the emotional and moral debt of the past is reduced, which at least partially rebalances the ledger.

When we undo what we've done, we improve our current situation. That helps. But undoing a regret is not quite the same as erasing it. Jeff Bosley told me that even after many tattoo removal sessions, the words on his left arm are impossible to read, but they haven't fully disappeared. "It almost looks like a light bruise now," he says.

So, to address regrets of action, begin by asking yourself these questions:

- If I've harmed others, as is often the case with moral regrets and sometimes the case with connection regrets, can I make amends through an apology or some form of emotional or material restitution?

- If I've harmed myself, as is the case for many foundation regrets and some connection regrets, can I fix the mistake? For example, can I begin paying down debt or logging a few more hours at work? Can I reach out immediately to someone whose connection I severed?

If the action regret can be undone, try to do that—even if a light physical or metaphysical bruise remains. But if it can't be undone, fear not. You've got another possibility.

STEP 2. *AT LEAST* IT

The other way to address the present is not to repair our previous actions but to recast the way we think about them. Let me offer an example from my own life.

Thirty years ago, nearly fresh out of college, I went to law school. I regret it. It wasn't a calamity. It was just a poor decision. If only I'd made a wiser choice, perhaps by waiting longer or by choosing an entirely different trajectory, I could have devoted those years to endeavors more fulfilling and better for the world—and I would have struggled less in the early years of my working life. But I also met my wife in law school, which was a glorious triumph for my well-being. I can't undo an action regret like this. But one way to ease its sting is to switch from *If Only* to *At Least*. Going to law school was a mistake—but *at least* I met my wife.

At Leasts don't alter our behavior or boost our performance in the future, but they do help us reassess the present. For instance, several women in the World Regret Survey listed marrying a previous husband as their greatest regret. But those who were mothers also cherished the children who came from that ill-considered marriage.

"I regret marrying a loser," they would say, "but at least I've got these great kids." Finding a silver lining doesn't negate the existence of a cloud. But it does offer another perspective on that cloud.

And while *At Leasts* can be useful for significant regrets like misguided marriage choices, they are especially helpful for addressing peskier regrets that fall outside the big four categories. For example, suppose that you recently bought a new car, but now you regret the decision and wish you'd purchased a different make and model. Assuming the car is safe and functional, the exact type of car you drive has little bearing on your enduring happiness and satisfaction. In fact, whatever car we own, plain or swanky, we get used to it pretty quickly.[3] So while you might try to find a future-facing lesson from the regret—next time check the consumer guides more carefully before purchasing a vehicle—you should also *At Least* it. Think about how it could have turned out worse. "At least I got a good deal." "At least I didn't buy that other make and model, which had less trunk space." "At least it's paid off."

At Leasts can turn regret into relief. On their own they don't change our behavior, but they change how we feel about our behavior, which can be valuable. And because *At Leasts* spring to mind naturally far less often than *If Onlys*, we must summon them ourselves at the right time. *At Leasts* work like antibiotics. Sometimes we need to reach into the medicine cabinet and pop a few of them to fortify our psychological immune system and fight off certain harmful emotions.[4] If we use these antibiotics too often, their efficacy will wane. If we use them intelligently, they can aid in healthy functioning.

So, with action regrets that are bringing you down, ask yourself:

- How could the decision I now regret have turned out worse?

- What is one silver lining in this regret?

- How would I complete the following sentence? "At least . . ."

As I was writing this book, Jeff was still working on undoing his regret through the slow and painful process of tattoo removal. It would require several more sessions and even more money.

At least he didn't choose a larger font.

"Ao longo da vida ter dedicado meu tempo aos estudos para a menta (racionals) e ter deixado de lado o conhecimento das emoções e sentimentos."*

Female, 40, Brazil

//

"I regret ignoring my inner voice and not heeding its plea to be more adventurous (moving country, changing job when the boss sucks) and for trying to live up to the expectations of society instead of focusing on myself."

Female, 47, Singapore

//

"I regret picking up a pack of Camel cigarettes on the way to a grim business meeting in 1999. To this day I smoke— sometimes heavily—out of habit more than enjoyment."

Male, 44, West Virginia

---

* "Throughout my life, I have devoted my time to studying the rational mind and have neglected understanding emotions and feelings."

13.

Disclosure, Compassion, and Distance

When last we met Cheryl Johnson, she was contending with a connection regret. She'd let a devoted friendship with Jen, a college classmate, drift apart over two decades, and she missed the closeness and camaraderie they'd once enjoyed. Hers is a regret of inaction, so she can't undo it; it's not possible to reverse a twenty-five-year void. She can't *At Least* it either. Saying "Our friendship evaporated, but at least we didn't have a huge fight" doesn't offer much solace or meaningfully adjust the present.

Cheryl's best response—and the optimal response to most regrets, action and inaction alike—is to use the regret to improve the future. If we look backward with the specific intent of moving forward, we can convert our regrets into fuel for progress. They can propel us toward smarter choices, higher performance, and greater meaning. And science shows us how.

Rather than ignoring the negative emotion of regret—or worse, wallowing in it—we can remember that feeling is for thinking and that thinking is for doing. Following a straightforward three-step process, we can disclose the regret, reframe the way we view it and ourselves, and extract a lesson from the experience to remake our subsequent decisions.

STEP 1. SELF-DISCLOSURE: RELIVE AND RELIEVE

Monkeys have constructed incredibly complex societies, but they have yet to establish a central bank that prints money and regulates its supply. Thus, when primatologists try to quantify what monkeys value, they introduce what they call a "liquid currency"—and what we non-primatologists call juice. By measuring how much fruit juice monkeys demand to behave the way researchers want, and how much they're willing to sacrifice to behave the way monkeys want, scientists can price primate priorities.

Robert Deaner, Amit Khera, and Michael Platt, previously at Duke University, helped develop the technique, and in 2005, they used it to measure how much a group of male macaques valued signals of status and sex. The experimenters discovered that if they wanted monkeys to look at photos of a low-status macaque, they had to bribe them with lots of juice. But photos of high-status monkeys and of female macaque hindquarters were so enticing that the monkeys were willing to *forgo* juice just to glimpse them. In other words, the monkeys required "liquid payment" to view unimportant monkeys but were willing to "pay" to look at powerful or attractive monkeys—all of which suggests that these animals place a high value on markers of dominance and sexual fitness.[1]

In 2012, the psychologists Diana Tamir, now at Princeton University, and Jason Mitchell, of Harvard University, used a modified version of this technique to assess what those macaques' close relatives—human beings—value most. In one study, Tamir and Mitchell presented their participants three choices: to reveal their beliefs about themselves, to judge the beliefs of other people, or to answer a trivia question. And they offered to pay varying amounts of money for each activity. Over 195 trials, people's preferences were clear. They *loved* talking about themselves—so much, in fact, that they were willing to take significantly less money for doing that than for any other behavior. "Just as monkeys are willing to forgo juice rewards to view dominant groupmates . . . individuals were willing to forgo money to disclose about the self," Tamir and Mitchell wrote.[2]

When Tamir and Mitchell then used functional magnetic resonance imaging to watch what was happening in the brains of these people, they saw that those who disclosed information about themselves had greater activation in the brain regions (the nucleus accumbens and the ventral tegmental area) that respond to food, money, and sex. The study, the researchers concluded, "provided both behavioral and neural evidence that self-disclosure is intrinsically rewarding."[3]

The first step in reckoning with all regrets, whether regrets of action or inaction, is self-disclosure. We're often skittish about revealing to others negative information about ourselves. It feels awkward, even shameful. But an enormous body of literature makes clear that disclosing our thoughts, feelings, and actions—by telling others or simply by writing about them—brings an array of physical, mental, and professional benefits. Such self-revelation is linked to reduced blood pressure, higher grades, better coping skills, and more.[4] Indeed, Tamir and Mitchell maintain that "our species may have an intrinsic drive to disclose thoughts to others."[5]

Self-disclosure is especially useful with regret. Denying our regrets taxes our minds and bodies. Gripping them too tightly can tip us into harmful rumination. The better approach is to *relive and relieve*. By divulging the regret, we reduce some of its burden, which can clear a path for making sense of it.

For example, psychologists like Sonja Lyubomirsky of the University of California, Riverside, have conducted studies that suggest people should process negative and positive experiences in different ways. In this research, writing about negative experiences like regret, and even talking into a tape recorder about them, for fifteen minutes a day substantially increased people's overall life satisfaction and improved their physical and mental well-being in ways that merely thinking about those experiences did not. Yet the reverse was true for positive experiences: writing and talking about triumphs and good times drained some of their positivity.[6]

The explanation—and the reason self-disclosure is so crucial for handling regret—is that language, whether written or spoken, forces us to organize and integrate our thoughts. It converts blobby mental abstractions into concrete linguistic units. That's a plus for negative emotions.[7]

Again, regret can make us better when we use emotions as a signal for our thoughts. When feeling is for thinking, and thinking is for doing, regret can perform its decision-enhancing, performance-boosting, meaning-deepening magic. Writing about regret or revealing a regret to another person moves the experience from the realm of emotion into the realm of cognition. Instead of those unpleasant feelings fluttering around uncontrollably, language helps us capture them in our net, pin them down, and begin analyzing them. By contrast, the same approach for positive experiences is less effective. For life's happy moments, avoiding analysis and sense-making helps us maintain the wonder and delight of those moments. Dissecting terrific events can diminish their terrificness.[8]

One misgiving we have with self-disclosure, particularly if we're revealing our previous failures to be prudent, trustworthy, or courageous, is that others will think poorly of us. But that is much less of a concern than we realize. One can go too far, of course. Oversharing intimate details about yourself can make others uneasy. But the evidence shows that self-disclosure builds affinity much more often than it triggers judgment. One major review of the literature concluded that "people who engage in intimate disclosures tend to be liked *more* than people who disclose at lower levels."[9]

Still, if you're squeamish about what others think of you, you needn't disclose your regret to anybody but yourself. The pathbreaking work of social psychologist James Pennebaker of the University of Texas, begun in the 1990s and expanded by him and other scholars for the last thirty years, has shown that merely writing about emotional difficulties, even solely for your own consumption, can be powerful. Among the benefits: fewer visits to physicians, long-term improvements in mood, strengthened immune function, better grades for students, finding jobs more quickly for the unemployed, and more.[10] In addition, Pennebaker has determined that these benefits extend widely: "The disclosure phenomenon appears to generalize across settings, many individual difference factors, and several Western cultures, and is independent of social feedback."[11]

The initial step in dealing with all forms of regret is to disclose the regret. Cheryl Johnson has done that—first by completing the

World Regret Survey, and then by talking with me about the strong friendship she had failed to maintain. In our conversation, she told me that she'd never told anyone the full tale of her experience and that brought a moment of clarity and a measure of relief.

Self-disclosure is intrinsically rewarding and extrinsically valuable. It can lighten our burden, make abstract negative emotions more concrete, and build affiliation. So, to begin to harness your regrets to improve in the future, try any of the following:

- Write about your regret for fifteen minutes for three consecutive days.

- Talk about your regret into a voice recorder for fifteen minutes for three consecutive days.

- Tell someone else about the regret in person or by phone. Include sufficient detail about what happened, but establish a time limit (perhaps a half hour) to avoid the possibilities of repetition and brooding.

STEP 2. SELF-COMPASSION: NORMALIZE AND NEUTRALIZE

After you disclose your regret, you are exposed—to yourself and others. And once exposed, you face a choice about how to respond. Do you dress yourself down? Or do you pump yourself up? Which is more effective—initiating a round of self-criticism or tapping your reserves of self-esteem?

The answer, it turns out, is neither.

As someone with an unbending commitment to self-criticism as well as a lifetime spent honing the technique, I was surprised when I went looking for evidence of its effectiveness. There isn't much. Self-criticism can sometimes motivate our performance when we criticize ourselves for particular actions rather than for deep-seated tendencies. But unless carefully managed and contained, self-criticism can become a form of inner-directed virtue signaling. It projects toughness and ambition, but often leads to rumination and hopelessness instead of productive action.[12]

Its opposite, self-esteem, can be more effective. Highly prized in certain parenting and education circles, where praise gushes and participation trophies gleam, self-esteem measures how much you value yourself. How good do you feel about who you are? How favorably do you evaluate your traits and behaviors? For example, in surveys, people with high self-esteem award themselves top marks for their looks, their brains, and their popularity—while people with low self-esteem make the opposite assessment. (Curiously, neither evaluation correlates with how smart, attractive, or popular someone actually is.)[13] We all need some baseline level of self-esteem to survive today and flourish tomorrow. And efforts to boost self-esteem can lift performance and lessen depression and anxiety.

But self-esteem brings downsides. Because it offers indiscriminate affirmation unconnected to genuine accomplishment, self-esteem can foster narcissism, diminish empathy, and stoke aggression. Criminals, for instance, have higher self-esteem than the general population. It can also promote bias toward one's own group and prejudice toward other groups.[14] Because self-esteem is comparative, to assess myself favorably, I often must denigrate others. These defects are why some of the finest social scientists of the last fifty years—among them, Edward Deci, Richard Ryan, and the late Albert Bandura—have long explored alternatives to self-esteem.

The most powerful and promising alternative—and the second

step in the regret-reckoning process—was pioneered nearly twenty years ago by University of Texas psychologist Kristin Neff. It is called "self-compassion."

Self-compassion emerged in part from Neff's recognition that when we stumble or fail, we treat ourselves more harshly than we would ever treat friends, family, or even strangers in the same predicament. That's counterproductive, she has shown. Rather than belittling or berating ourselves during moments of frustration and failure, we're better off extending ourselves the same warmth and understanding we'd offer another person. Self-compassion begins by replacing searing judgment with basic kindness. It doesn't ignore our screwups or neglect our weaknesses. It simply recognizes that "being imperfect, making mistakes, and encountering life difficulties is part of the shared human experience."[15] By *normalizing* negative experiences, we *neutralize* them. Self-compassion encourages us to take the middle road in handling negative emotions—not suppressing them, but not exaggerating or overidentifying with them either.

Self-compassion is also something that people can learn.[16] And when they master it, the benefits are considerable. Research by Neff and others has found that self-compassion is associated with increased optimism, happiness, curiosity, and wisdom;[17] enhanced personal initiative and emotional intelligence;[18] greater mental toughness;[19] and deeper social connections.[20] It can protect against unproductive mind-wandering,[21] and help students cope with academic failure.[22] It also correlates with less depression, anxiety, stress, perfectionism, and shame[23]—and reduces symptoms of posttraumatic stress disorder.[24] A 2019 meta-analysis of more than ninety studies showed that self-compassion can even promote better physical health, including improved immune function.[25]

In a sense, self-compassion delivers the benefits of self-esteem without its drawbacks. It can insulate us from the debilitating consequences of self-criticism, while short-circuiting self-esteem's need to feel good through vanity and comparison.

Its powers are especially evident with regret. In 2016, psychologists Jia Wei Zhang, now at the University of Memphis, and Serena Chen of the University of California, Berkeley, explored the effect that self-compassion has in helping people overcome and learn from their regrets. The researchers recruited several hundred participants and asked each of them to list their biggest regret.

Then they randomly divided participants into three groups. One group wrote a letter to themselves about their regret "from a compassionate and understanding perspective." The second group wrote a letter to themselves about the regret "from a perspective of validating your positive (rather than negative) qualities." The third group, which served as the control, wrote about a hobby they enjoyed.

The people who addressed their regret with self-compassion were more likely to change their behavior than those who approached their regret with self-esteem. Even this modest writing intervention led people to plan ways to avoid the behavior in the future—regardless of whether the regret involved action or inaction. "Self-compassion appears to orient people to embrace their regret," Zhang and Chen write, "and this willingness to remain in contact with their regret may afford people the opportunity to discover avenues for personal improvement."[26]

For a regret like Cheryl's, self-compassion doesn't mean exonerating herself for not making more of an effort to maintain her friendship. It means treating herself with the same graciousness she'd treat someone else who regretted a splintered friendship. It means "remaining in contact" with the regret, as Zhang and Chen put it, but not making the dissolved friendship the defining feature of her character. And it means moving past language like "I really screwed up," which Cheryl told me several times, and instead recognizing how normal, universal, and human her regret is.

A self-compassionate approach does not foster complacency, as some might fear.[27] While self-flagellation seems motivating— especially to Americans, whose mental models of motivation often begin with howling, red-faced, vein-popping football coaches—it often produces helplessness. Self-compassion, by contrast, prompts people to confront their difficulties head-on and take responsibility for them, researchers have found. As Neff writes, "Far from being an excuse for self-indulgence, therefore, self-compassion pushes us forward—and for the right reasons."[28]

So, drawing on the science of self-compassion, the second step in transforming our regrets is to ask ourselves three questions:

- If a friend or relative came to you with the same regret as yours, would you treat that person with kindness or contempt? If your answer is kindness, use that approach on yourself. If your answer is contempt, try a different answer.

- Is this type of regret something that other people might have endured, or are you the only person ever to have experienced it? If you believe your stumble is part of our common humanity, reflect on that belief, as it's almost always true. If you believe the world has it out for you alone, please reread Chapters 7–10.

- Does this regret represent an unpleasant moment in your life, or does it define your life? Again, if you believe it's worth being aware of the regret but not overidentifying with it, you're on your way. If you believe this regret fully constitutes who you are, ask someone else what they think.

These three questions, which form the heart of self-compassion, bring us to the last step of the process.

STEP 3. SELF-DISTANCING: ANALYZE AND STRATEGIZE

On the surface at least, Julius Caesar and Elmo make an unlikely pair. One was a Roman statesman, general, and historian who was immortalized in a Shakespeare play and who lived more than two thousand years ago. The other is a slightly manic Muppet with mangy red fur and an orange nose, whose exact citizenship is unclear but whose last forwarding address was Sesame Street.

Yet both of these figures are expert practitioners of the same rhetorical maneuver: "illeism," a fancy word for talking about oneself in the third person. When Julius Caesar describes his Gallic Wars exploits in his book *Commentarii de Bello Gallico*, he never uses "I" or other first-person pronouns. Instead, he crafts sentences like, "Caesar learned through spies that the mountain was in possession of his own men." Likewise, when Elmo explains his commitment to the life of the mind, he, too, disdains the first person. He favors constructions like "Elmo loves to learn!"

Some people find illeism annoying (although it doesn't bother Daniel Pink). But its existence as a style of speech and narration exemplifies the final step in the regret-reckoning process. Talking about ourselves in the third person is one variety of what social psychologists call "self-distancing."

When we're beset by negative emotions, including regret, one response is to immerse ourselves in them, to face the negativity by getting up close and personal. But immersion can catch us in an undertow of rumination. A better, more effective, and longer-lasting approach is to move in the opposite direction—not to plunge in, but to zoom out and gaze upon our situation as a detached observer, much as a movie director pulls back the camera.

After self-disclosure relieves the burden of carrying a regret, and self-compassion reframes the regret as a human imperfection rather than an incapacitating flaw, self-distancing helps you *analyze and strategize*—to examine the regret dispassionately without shame or rancor and to extract from it a lesson that can guide your future behavior.

Self-distancing changes your role from scuba diver to oceanographer, from swimming in the murky depths of regret to piloting above the water to examine its shape and shoreline. "People who self-distance focus less on recounting their experiences and more on reconstruing them in ways that provide insight and closure," explain Ethan Kross of the University of Michigan and Özlem Ayduk of the University of California, Berkeley, two prominent scholars of the subject.[29] Shifting from the immersive act of recounting to the more distanced act of reconstruing regulates our emotions and redirects behavior. As a result, self-distancing strengthens thinking,[30] enhances problem-solving skills,[31] deepens wisdom,[32] and even reduces the elevated blood pressure that often accompanies stressful situations.[33]

We can create distance from our regrets in three ways.

First, we can distance through space. The classic move is known, unsurprisingly, as the "fly-on-the-wall technique." Rather than examine your regret from your own perspective—"I really screwed up by letting my close friendship with Jen come apart and then doing nothing to fix it"—view the scene from the perspective of a neutral observer. "I watched a person let an important friendship drift. But all of us make mistakes, and she can redeem this one by reaching out to meaningful connections, including Jen, more regularly and more often."

You may have noticed that you're often better at solving other people's problems than your own. Because you're less enmeshed in others' details than they are, you're able to see the full picture in ways they cannot. In fact, Kross and Igor Grossmann of Canada's University of Waterloo have shown that when people step back and assess their own situation the way they'd evaluate other people's situations, they close this perceptual gap. They reason as effectively about their own problems as they do about others' problems.[34] Equally important, the fly-on-the-wall technique helps us withstand and learn from criticism—it makes it easier not to take it personally—which is essential in transforming regrets into instruments for improvement.[35] This sort of distancing can be physical as well as mental. Going to a different location to analyze the regret or even literally leaning back, rather than forward, in one's chair can make challenges seem less difficult and reduce anxiety in addressing them.[36]

The second way to self-distance is through time. We can enlist the same capacity for time travel that gives birth to regret to analyze and strategize about learning from these regrets. For example, one study showed that prompting people to consider how they might feel about a negative situation in ten years reduced their stress and enhanced their problem-solving capabilities compared to contemplating what the situation would be like in a week.[37]

Mentally visiting the future—and then examining the regret retrospectively—activates a similar type of detached, big-picture perspective as the fly-on-the-wall technique. It can make the problem seem smaller, more temporary, and easier to surmount.[38] Cheryl, for instance, could envision how she'd react a decade from now, peering back on her regret. Does she feel bad about letting the friendship remain apart for thirty-five years? Or does she feel satisfied that she addressed her connection regrets—with Jen or with others? When we simulate looking at the problem retrospectively, from the binoculars of tomorrow rather than the magnifying glass of today, we're more likely to replace self-justification with self-improvement.[39]

The third method of self-distancing, as Julius Caesar and Elmo teach us, is through language. Kross, Ayduk, and others have carried out some fascinating research concluding that "subtle shifts in the language people use to refer to themselves during introspection can influence their capacity to regulate how they think, feel, and behave under stress."[40] When we abandon the first person in talking to ourselves, the distance that creates can help us recast threats as challenges and replace distress with meaning. For example, borrowing a page from Caesar, Grossmann and several colleagues found that getting people to write about their challenges using third-person pronouns like "she," "him," and "they" rather than first-person pronouns like "I," "me," and "my" increased their intellectual humility and sharpened the way they reasoned through difficulties.[41] Addressing regrets in the second person—referring to oneself as "you" rather than "I"—also strengthens people's behavior and deepens their commitment to improving future behavior, according to research by Sanda Dolcos and Dolores Albarracín.[42] Similarly, deploying what some call the "universal you"—using "you" to mean people in general—can destigmatize negative experiences and help people pull meaning from them.[43]

And Elmo might be wiser than he looks. Addressing yourself by your name has similar effects. For example, another Kross-led project found that during the 2014 Ebola scare, people who were randomly assigned to use their own name, rather than "I," in thinking about the disease were better able to generate fact-based reasons not to panic about the outbreak.[44] Equally important, self-distancing through language is neither laborious nor time-consuming. According to one neuroimaging study, its effects can kick in within one second.[45]

So, to gain the benefits of self-distancing, try any of the following:

- Imagine your best friend is confronting the same regret that you're dealing with. What is the lesson that the regret teaches them? What would you tell them to do next? Be as specific as you can. Now follow your own advice.

- Imagine that you are a neutral expert—a doctor of regret sciences—analyzing your regret in a clean, pristine examination room. What is your diagnosis? Explain in clinical terms what went wrong. Next, what is your prescription? Now write an email to yourself— using your first name and the pronoun "you"— outlining the small steps you need to learn from the regret.

- If your regret involves your business or career, try a technique from the late Intel CEO Andy Grove, who reportedly would ask himself, "If I were replaced tomorrow, what would my successor do?"[46]

- Imagine it is ten years from now and you're looking back with pride on how you responded to this regret. What did you do?

Looking backward can move us forward, but only if we do it right. The sequence of self-disclosure, self-compassion, and self-distancing offers a simple yet systematic way to transform regret into a powerful force for stability, achievement, and purpose.

B ut we're still not quite done. It's also possible to move forward by *looking forward*—by foreseeing regrets before they occur.

SEVEN OTHER TECHNIQUES
YOU WON'T REGRET

1. Start a regret circle.

Think of regret circles as close cousins of book clubs. Gather
five or six friends over coffee, tea, or drinks. Ask two of them to
come prepared with a significant regret. Let them tell the story
of their regrets. Have the others respond to each regret first by
categorizing it. (Is it action or inaction? Into which, if any, of
the four deep structure categories does it fall?) Then, for each
regret, the group works through the Disclosure-Compassion-
Distance process. When the gathering ends, the two people
commit to adopting a specific behavior (for example, speaking
up to an unpleasant boss or asking out a crush). At the next
meeting, the others hold the regretters accountable for that
promise—and two new people share their regrets.

2. Create a failure résumé.

Most of us have a résumé—a written compendium of jobs,
experiences, and credentials that demonstrate to prospective
employers and clients how qualified, adept, and generally
awesome we are. Tina Seelig, a professor of practice at Stanford
University, says we also need a "failure résumé," a detailed and
thorough inventory of our flops. A failure résumé offers
another method for addressing our regrets. The very act of
creating one is a form of disclosure. And by eyeing your failure
résumé not as its protagonist, but as an observer, you can learn
from it without feeling diminished by your mistakes. A few
years ago, I compiled a failure résumé, then tried to glean
lessons from the many screwups I'd committed. (Disclosing
these embarrassments to myself will be sufficient, thank you

very much.) I realized I'd repeatedly made variations of the same two mistakes, and that knowledge has helped me avoid those mistakes again.

3. Study self-compassion.

I've been reading social science research and attempting to make sense of it for twenty years now, but few subjects have spoken to me as powerfully as the research on self-compassion. Understanding self-compassion helped me curb excessive self-criticism because I became convinced that berating myself, while masochistically enjoyable, just wasn't effective. Self-compassion similarly helped me see my idiosyncratic struggles as both common and solvable. I encourage you to look more deeply into this topic. One place to begin is Kristin Neff's website (https://self-compassion.org), where you can measure your own levels of self-compassion. Her book *Self-Compassion: The Proven Power of Being Kind to Yourself* is also excellent.

4. Pair New Year's resolutions with Old Year's regrets.

A core point of this chapter—of this entire book—is that looking backward can move us forward. One way to imprint this principle onto your life is to establish a ritual. In late December, the temporal landmark of January 1 stirs us to make New Year's resolutions. But as a precursor to that practice, try what I call "Old Year's regrets." Look back on the year that's about to end and list three regrets. Do you regret not reconnecting with a relative or former colleague? Or never getting around to launching that side business? Or telling a lie that compromised your values? Write down these regrets. And make undoing the action regrets and transforming the inaction regrets your top resolutions for the new year.

5. Mentally subtract positive events.

To take the hurt out of a regret, try a mental trick made famous in the 1946 movie *It's a Wonderful Life*. On Christmas Eve, George Bailey stands on the brink of suicide when he's visited by Clarence, an angel who shows George what life in Bedford Falls would be like had he never been born. Clarence's technique is called "mentally subtracting positive events."[47] Think of something good in your life—a close friendship, a career achievement, one of your children. Consider all the decisions and indecisions, mistakes and triumphs, that led to that happy situation. Now take them away. To use an example from the last chapter, I could mentally subtract having met my wife. The result is misery and gloom. But, as happened with George Bailey, the subtraction deepens my gratitude and casts my regrets in a new light.

6. Participate in the World Regret Survey.

If you haven't done so already, submit your regret to the World Regret Survey (www.worldregretsurvey.com). Putting your regret in writing can defang it—and can offer the distance to evaluate it and plan from it. You can also read other people's regrets, which provides perspective on our shared humanity and can help strengthen your regret-reckoning muscles. As you read regrets from across the globe, ask yourself: What kind of regret is this? What advice would you give the writer for using her regret as a positive force?

7. Adopt a journey mindset.

Achieving our goals can insulate us from regret. But if we don't sustain our behavior after reaching those goals—by continuing to exercise regularly or by maintaining the good work habits that led to the completion of a project—regret quickly finds its way into our minds. One antidote to this problem comes from the work of Stanford University professors Szu-chi Huang and Jennifer Aaker, who recommend what they call a "journey mindset." Huang and Aaker have found that when we reach a destination—when we've completed a difficult and important task—we sometimes slack off and assume our work is done. But it's usually not. Don't just relish the goal you've achieved. Review the steps that got you there. Spend less time celebrating the destination and more time contemplating the journey.

"I regret that I let a college counselor convince me that I didn't have what it takes to be a doctor. I wish I had believed in myself and at least tried."

Female, 54, Maryland

//

"I regret wasting so much free time before having children. In hindsight, I absolutely WAS NOT too busy to learn Spanish, exercise regularly, or put in extra effort at work to attain mastery."

Male, 29, Indiana

//

"Not being more sexually active."

Female, 71, Michigan

14.

Anticipating Regret

"Live as if you were living already for the
second time and as if you had acted the first time
as wrongly as you are about to act now!"

Viktor Frankl, 1946

One morning in 1888, Alfred Nobel awoke to a surprise in the morning newspaper. On the pages of the publication, in black and white for all to read, was his obituary. A French journalist had mistaken Alfred's brother, Ludvig, who had died, for Alfred, who most assuredly had not. It was fake news for the fin de siècle set.

But what really rankled Alfred was how the obituary's headline encapsulated his life's work: *"Le marchand de la mort est mort"* ("The merchant of death is dead").

Nobel, a Swede who spoke five languages, was an ingenious chemist and an accomplished inventor. And what he invented were things that went boom: detonators, blasting caps, and, most famously, dynamite, which he patented in the 1860s. He built dynamite factories all over the world, which made him a multimillionaire and one of Europe's most prominent industrialists.

Yet the obit didn't tell a story of technical genius and entrepreneurial pluck. It described a contaminated soul with a shameful legacy—a greedy and amoral man who became fabulously wealthy by selling people tools for obliterating each other.

Eight years later, when Nobel did die, his will contained a surprise. Instead of leaving his fortune to his family, his estate established a set of prizes for "those who, during the preceding year, shall have conferred the greatest benefit on mankind"—the Nobel Prizes.

The impetus for this gesture, the legend goes, was that premature obituary.[1] Nobel glimpsed a preview of his future and he regretted what he saw. Anticipating this regret, he changed his behavior to avoid it.

If the previous two chapters were about regret through the rearview mirror, this chapter is about regret through the front windshield. Regret is a retrospective emotion. It springs into being when we look backward. But we can also use it prospectively and proactively—to gaze into the future, predict what we will regret, and then reorient our behavior based on our forecast. Sometimes that approach points us in a promising direction. Other times it can lead us astray. But if we understand both the upside and downside of anticipating regret, we can hone our strategy for pursuing the good life.

THE UPSIDE OF ANTICIPATION

Like most large research institutions, Duke University operates an extensive library system that serves its students, faculty, and staff. And like most organizations of any kind, Duke University Libraries wants to know what its customers and constituents think of its offerings. To assess opinion and gather feedback, DUL traditionally relied on surveys emailed to its community. But it faced a perennial problem: most people didn't bother completing those questionnaires.

So, the crafty librarians of Duke hatched a plan—a simple experiment that sheds light on anticipated regret.

In 2016, DUL sent half of Duke's six thousand undergraduates a survey and told them that if they completed and returned it, they'd be entered into a raffle for a $75 gift card.

The other three thousand students also received an email with the survey. But the accompanying rules were different. *Everybody* would be entered in a raffle for a $75 gift card. But if the organizers drew someone's name and that person had not completed the survey, he would be ineligible for the prize and the organizers would select another name.

Which approach yielded the most survey responses?

It wasn't even close. Within a week, only one-third of the students in the first group had completed the survey, but two-thirds of the students in the second group had done so.[2] The first instance was a good old-fashioned raffle. The second was what behavioral economists have come to call a "regret lottery."

Regret lotteries are one way that anticipated regrets can alter our behavior. With an ordinary lottery, I must take affirmative steps to enter—in the Duke example, by filling out the questionnaire and returning it. If I don't do that and someone who does ends up winning, I might be slightly bummed out (assuming I even find out). But with the odds slim and my emotional investment almost nonexistent, I'm unlikely to be devastated.

However, with a regret lottery, I evaluate my decision differently. If the organizers draw my name, and I haven't completed the survey, I know I'll kick myself. I can readily envision a future where I win the prize—but the gift card is snatched from my hands because of my own stupidity, laziness, or lack of effort. And if I anticipate that sinking feeling, I'll proceed like two-thirds of those Blue Devils and complete the questionnaire.

Regret lotteries have been effective in changing behavior in many domains.[3] They exploit a cognitive quirk similar to "loss aversion." In general, we find the pain of losing something greater than the pleasure of gaining the equivalent thing—so we go to extraordinary (and often irrational) lengths to avoid losses. "Losses loom larger than gains," the dictum goes.[4] Similarly, when we anticipate our emotions, regret looms larger than rejoicing. In many situations, the prospective pain of regret outweighs the prospective gain of the alternative.

That can often work to our advantage. Anticipating our regrets slows our thinking. It applies our cerebral brakes, giving us time to gather additional information and to reflect before we decide what to do. Anticipated regret is particularly useful in overcoming regrets of inaction.

For instance, during the coronavirus pandemic, the largest predictor of young adults getting a COVID test was the regret they said they'd feel from not acting—if they avoided the test and then accidently passed the virus to someone else—according to a 2021 study by Russell Ravert of the University of Missouri, Linda Fu of Children's National Hospital in Washington, DC, and Gregory Zimet of the Indiana University School of Medicine.[5] Another

2021 study, conducted by Katharina Wolff of the University of Bergen in Norway, found a similar effect with COVID vaccines. The anticipated inaction regret of not getting vaccinated, and thus endangering oneself and others, was a more powerful force in prompting people to get vaccinated than even factors like what one's peers and family had chosen to do.[6]

When we envision how awful we might feel in the future if we don't act appropriately now, that negative emotion—which we simulate rather than experience—can improve our behavior. A 2016 meta-analysis of eighty-one studies involving 45,618 participants found that "anticipated regret was associated with a broad array of health behaviors."[7] For example, one well-regarded British study by Charles Abraham of the University of Sussex and Paschal Sheeran of the University of Sheffield showed that people prompted to agree with the simple statement, "If I did not exercise at least six times in the next two weeks, I would feel regret," ended up exercising significantly more than people for whom regret was not on their minds.[8]

A pile of studies over the last fifteen years has demonstrated that anticipating regret can also prompt us to: eat more fruits and vegetables,[9] get an HPV vaccine,[10] sign up for a flu shot,[11] use condoms,[12] seek more information about our health,[13] look for early signs of cancer,[14] drive more carefully,[15] get a cervical screening,[16] quit smoking,[17] reduce consumption of processed foods,[18] and even recycle more.[19]

Anticipating regret offers a convenient tool for judgment. In situations where you're unsure of your next move, ask yourself, "In the future, will I regret this decision if I don't do X?" Answer the question. Apply that answer to your current situation. This approach underlies the (small but growing) popularity of "obituary parties"—in which people channel their inner Alfred Nobel, draft their own obits, and use the written pieces to inform their remaining years.[20] It is also the animating idea of "pre-mortems." In this management technique, work teams mentally travel to the future before a project even begins to imagine a nightmare scenario where everything went wrong—say, the project came in over time or over budget or didn't even get done. Then they use those insights to avoid the blunders before they occur.[21]

If one person embodies this approach to work and life—the apex predator of the anticipated regret food chain—that person is Jeff Bezos. He's one of the richest people in the world, thanks to founding Amazon, one of the largest companies on the planet. He owns *The Washington Post*. He visits outer space. Yet in the domain of our most misunderstood emotion, he is best known for a concept that he calls the "Regret Minimization Framework."

In the early 1990s, Bezos was working in banking when he conceived a company that would sell books via a newfangled technology called the World Wide Web. When Bezos told his boss that he intended to leave his high-paying job, the boss urged him to think about the move for a few days before committing.

A computer scientist by training, Bezos wanted a systematic way to analyze his decision—an algorithm of sorts for reaching a sound conclusion. And he finally came up with it. As he explained in a 2001 interview:

> I wanted to project myself forward to age 80 and say, "Okay, now I'm looking back on my life. I want to have minimized the number of regrets I have." I knew that when I was 80 I was not going to regret having tried this. I was not going to regret trying to participate in this thing called the Internet that I thought was going to be a really big deal. I knew that if I failed I wouldn't regret that, but I knew the one thing I might regret

is not ever having tried. I knew that that would haunt me every day, and so, when I thought about it that way it was an incredibly easy decision.[22]

Bezos anticipated a boldness regret, then made avoiding it in the future the impetus for his behavior in the present. The Regret Minimization Framework was a wise move for him, and it's a useful mental model for the rest of us. Anticipating our regrets, we've seen, can improve our health, help us become billionaires, and earn the affection of survey-distributing college librarians. It is a powerful medicine.

But it should come with a warning label.

THE DOWNSIDE OF ANTICIPATION

To understand how anticipated regrets can go sideways, let me invite you to ride a subway, buy a microwave oven, exchange a Powerball ticket, and take a standardized test.

Imagine it's the morning rush hour and you're racing to catch a subway train to work. On your way to the station, your shoe comes untied because in your earlier rush you tied it so hastily. You find an empty patch of sidewalk, stop for a minute, retie your shoe, and move on. As you arrive on the subway platform, you see your train pull away. Drat! If only you hadn't stopped to fix your laces, you would have made your train.

How much regret would you anticipate experiencing from missing the train by one minute?

And a related question: How much regret would you expect to experience if instead you missed the train by five minutes?

According to Daniel Gilbert of Harvard University, who led a group of researchers who conducted experiments about this very issue at a subway station in Cambridge, Massachusetts, most people forecast that they'll suffer much greater regret from the one-minute miss than the five-minute miss. Yet in reality, the amount of regret people actually endure is about the same in both situations, and it turns out to be not very much at all.

One problem with using anticipated regrets as a decision-making tool is that we're pretty bad at predicting the intensity and duration of our emotions.[23] And we're particularly inept at predicting regret. We often overestimate how negative we'll feel and underestimate our capacity to cope or balm our feelings with *At Leasts*. As Gilbert and his colleagues write, anticipated regret "can be a bit of a boogeyman, looking larger in prospect than it actually stands in experience." We're like bumbling meteorologists who keep (mis)predicting rain. As a result, the researchers say, "decision makers who pay to avoid future regrets may be buying emotional insurance that they do not actually need."[24]

Overestimating regret has another consequence: it can cloud our decisions. Suppose that after waiting a bit, you've boarded the next train and made it to work. After a productive morning, you take a lunch break and walk to a nearby electronics store to purchase a countertop microwave oven for your apartment. After a brief conversation with the salesperson, you narrow the options to two.

Both ovens are the same size, deliver the same power, and offer the same features. They appear identical except in two respects. The first microwave is from a well-known brand; the second is from a generic brand. And the first microwave costs $149, while the second costs $109.

Which do you choose?

When Itamar Simonson of Stanford University conducted an

experiment like this, he found that consumers split about fifty-fifty. Half chose the more expensive name brand; half chose the less expensive generic brand.

But then he introduced a wrinkle. He told buyers that shortly after they made their decision, he'd reveal how an independent consumer magazine rated the two choices. With that promise in the air, the buyers grew cautious. More people—two-thirds, in fact—selected the name brand. People anticipated greater regret if they departed from the status quo (opting for the recognized brand) and then learned it was the wrong decision.[25] So, to bypass that unpleasant sensation, the buyers played it safe. They became less concerned with making the smarter choice and tried to make the less regrettable choice—and those aren't always the same.

Anticipating regret can sometimes steer us away from the best decision and toward the decision that most shields us from regret—as you'll discover again when you return to the office.

After leaving the electronics store, you buy a $1 ticket for to-morrow evening's $80 million Powerball drawing. As it happens, I've also bought a Powerball ticket. And I decide to make you a deal. I offer to trade you my ticket for yours—and give you $3 for it.

Would you accept?

Of course, you should. And, of course, you won't.

Both of our tickets have an equal chance of winning. If you make the exchange, your odds of winning Powerball remain iden-tical and extremely remote. But you'll now have three more dollars than before. It's a no-brainer!

But in laboratory experiments, more than half of people resist such offers—because it's so easy to imagine the regret they'll feel if they traded away the eventual winner.[26] Only when exper-imenters place the lottery ticket in a sealed envelope—so people can't see their original numbers and won't know if they held the winning ticket—are people more willing to make this type of exchange.[27]

In the Powerball case and many others, minimizing regret is not the same as minimizing risk. And if we don't anticipate properly, we end up making the regret-minimizing choice rather than the risk-minimizing choice. Sometimes that means no decision at all. Regret aversion can often lead to decision aversion, many studies have shown.[28] If we focus too much on what we'll regret, we can freeze and decide not to decide. Likewise, in studies of negotiation, focusing too much on anticipated regret actually stalled progress. It made negotiators risk averse and less likely to strike a deal.[29]

Your workday is nearing an end, but your obligations are not. Because you're an ambitious sort, you're also studying for a real estate license along with holding down your current job. Tonight is your first exam—eighty multiple-choice questions.

You gulp a cup of coffee and enter the exam room. You've got two hours to complete the exam. It's going well. You're proceeding steadily through the questions, marking your answers on the bubble form, when a thought occurs to you.

"On question twenty-three, I chose B. But now I think that C might be the right answer."

Do you return to that question, erase your original response, and pencil in a new one? Or do you stick with your first instinct?

At every level of schooling and professional training, the advice that experts offer is consistent. In surveys, most college professors suggest that you stay with your initial instinct, because changing answers typically hurts student grades. The academic advisers at Penn State University concur: "[Y]our first hunch is usually correct. Don't change an answer unless you are very sure of the change." The Princeton Review, whose business is preparing students for every variety of standardized test, cautions: "Most times you want to go with your gut, rather than over thinking your answers. Many students just end up changing the right answer to the wrong one!"[30]

The conventional wisdom is plain: stick with your first instinct and don't change the answer.

The conventional wisdom is also wrong. Nearly every study conducted on the topic has shown that when students change answers on tests, they are significantly more likely to change from a wrong answer to a right answer (sweet!) than they are to switch from a right answer to a wrong one (d'oh!). Students who change their answers usually improve their scores.[31]

So, why does this wrongheaded advice endure?

Anticipated regret distorts our judgment.

In 2005, Justin Kruger, a social psychologist now at New York University, along with Derrick Wirtz, now at the University of British Columbia, and Dale Miller of Stanford University examined the erasures on more than 1,500 psychology exams taken by students at the University of Illinois, where Kruger and Wirtz were then teaching. Consistent with previous research, switches from the wrong answer to the right answer were twice as common as switches from right to wrong.

But when researchers asked the students which they would anticipate regretting more—"switching when I should have stuck" or "sticking when I should have switched"—the responses were revealing. Seventy-four percent of those students anticipated more regret from switching answers. Twenty-six percent said it wouldn't matter. And exactly none of the students anticipated greater regret from sticking with their initial answer.

Kruger, Wirtz, and Miller call this the "first instinct fallacy," and it grows from anticipated regret gone awry. "Getting a problem wrong as a result of going against one's first instinct is more memorable than getting a problem wrong because of failing to go against one's first instinct," they write. "The regret produced by switching an answer when one should have stuck with one's original answer is enough to make the misfortune of having missed the question seem almost tragic."[32] Haunted by the prospective specter of *If Only*, we err. You err, too. Because you didn't switch your answer, you just missed passing the test and must take it again. If only you knew about this research earlier.

Anticipated regret—AR—can often make us better. But as your eventful day demonstrates, before you take this medicine, read the label.

<u>**Warning:**</u>
AR may cause decision paralysis, risk aversion,
first instinct fallacies, and lower test scores.

As a universal drug, anticipated regret has a few dangerous side effects. But that's not its only problem.

Herbert Simon is one of the nearly one thousand people who've won the prize named for the regret-anticipating dynamite mogul we met earlier in this chapter. Simon was a masterful social scientist who taught at Carnegie Mellon University for fifty years and whose intellectual contributions spanned many fields, including political science, cognitive psychology, and artificial intelligence. But perhaps his greatest legacy was pushing the field of economics to consider the human dimension in its analyses.

In the pre-Simon world, the dominant economic models assumed that when people made decisions, their preferences were stable and they had all the information they needed, so they always tried to maximize their outcomes. In every instance, and at every moment, we sought to buy at the lowest price possible, sell at the highest price, and relentlessly maximize our gains.

Simon persuaded the economics profession that this assumption, while accurate in some cases, wasn't always correct. Our preferences sometimes changed. Depending on a variety of factors, we often lacked the proper information to make the ideal decision. Besides, pursuing the very best deal everywhere in our lives could be exhausting. In many situations, we simply didn't care sufficiently to find the perfect option—the ideal roofer, the peerless fast-food burger—and were willing to settle for good enough.

Sometimes we maximize, Simon explained. Other times we "satisfice."[33] If this were true—and analyses of people's behavior showed that it is—the models had to change—and they did. For his work, in 1978 Simon won the Nobel Memorial Prize for Economic Sciences.

It took a while for psychologists to begin exploring the emotional consequences of Simon's two decision-making approaches. But that moment arrived in 2002 when six social scientists, led by Barry Schwartz and Andrew Ward of Swarthmore College, developed a personality scale that measured an individual's propensity to maximize or satisfice. Using a set of seventeen questions, they were able to identify which people pursued ideal standards (the maximizers) and which more often selected whatever met some threshold of acceptability (the satisficers.)

After administering their Maximization Scale to more than 1,700 participants, they connected the results to measures of these participants' well-being. And the researchers uncovered a surprise. Most maximizers were miserable. The maximizers reported "significantly less life satisfaction, happiness, [and] optimism" and significantly more depression than the satisficers.[34]

When the scientists tried to explain the source of the unhappiness, they identified the main culprit: "maximizers' increased sensitivity to regret—both experienced and anticipated." Maximizers regretted everything at every stage. Before they made their choices. After they made their choices. While they made their choices. Whatever the situation, they always imagined the possibilities of something better if only they had acted differently.[35] But these upward counterfactuals didn't uncork productive "feeling is for thinking" regret. They trapped people in ruminating "feeling is for feeling" regret. In their effort to maximize happiness on all things, they were pulverizing it on most things.

And herein lies a problem. The wobbly beam in Bezos's Regret Minimization Framework is that constantly trying to anticipate and minimize our regrets can become a form of unhealthy maximizing. Applying this framework at all times and in all realms is a recipe for despair.

How, then, to reconcile these countervailing currents—to gain the benefits of anticipated regret without becoming caught in its downdraft?

The solution is to focus our aspirations.

OPTIMIZING REGRET

Our goal should not be to always minimize regret. Our goal should be to *optimize* it. By combining the science of anticipated regret with the new deep structure of regret, we can refine our mental model.

Call it the Regret Optimization Framework.

This revised framework is built on four principles:

- In many circumstances, anticipating our regrets can lead to healthier behavior, smarter professional choices, and greater happiness.

- Yet when we anticipate our regrets, we frequently overestimate them, buying emotional insurance we don't need and thereby distorting our decisions.

- And if we go too far—if we maximize on regret minimization—we can make our situation even worse.

- At the same time, people around the world consistently express the same four core regrets. These regrets endure. They reveal fundamental human needs. And together, they offer a path to the good life.

The Regret Optimization Framework holds that we should devote time and effort to anticipate the four core regrets: foundation regrets, boldness regrets, moral regrets, and connection regrets. But anticipating regrets outside these four categories is usually not worthwhile.

So, under the Regret Optimization Framework, when deciding a course of action, begin by asking whether you are dealing with one of the four core regrets.

If not, satisfice. For example, if you're buying lawn furniture or a(nother) microwave oven, that decision is unlikely to involve any fundamental, enduring human need. Make a choice and move on. You'll be fine.

If the decision does involve one of the big four, spend more time deliberating. Project yourself into the future—five years, ten years, at age eighty, whatever makes sense. From that future vantage point, ask yourself which choice will help you build your foundation, take a sensible risk, do the right thing, or maintain a meaningful connection. Anticipate these regrets. Then choose the option that most reduces them. Use this framework a few times, and you will begin to see its power.

Our everyday lives consist of hundreds of decisions—some of them crucial to our well-being, many of them inconsequential. Understanding the difference can make all the difference. If we know what we truly regret, we know what we truly value. Regret—that maddening, perplexing, and undeniably real emotion—points the way to a life well lived.

WHAT TO DO WITH YOUR REGRETS:
A RECAP

For an Action Regret

1. **Undo it.** Apologize, make amends, or try to repair the damage.

2. **At Least It.** Find the silver lining: think about how the situation could have turned out worse and appreciate that it didn't.

For Any Regret (Action or Inaction)

1. **Self-disclosure.** Relive and relieve the regret by telling others about it—admission clears the air—or by writing about it privately.

2. **Self-compassion.** Normalize and neutralize the regret by treating yourself the way you'd treat a friend.

3. **Self-distancing.** Analyze and strategize about the lessons you've learned from the regret by zooming out in time, in space, or through language.

To Use Anticipated Regrets in Your Decision Making:

1. **Satisfice on most decisions.** If you are *not* dealing with one of the four core regrets, make a choice, don't second-guess yourself, and move on.

2. **Maximize on the most crucial decisions.** If you *are* dealing with one of the four core regrets, project yourself to a specific point in the future and ask yourself which choice will most help you build a solid foundation, take a sensible risk, do the right thing, or connect with others.

"I regret that I wasn't braver and that I didn't do more to uphold our democracy!"

Female, 82, Pennsylvania

//

"I regret not being kinder to people. I was too often concerned with being 'right' instead of being kind."

Male, 41, United Kingdom

//

"Not going to see Prince in concert because it was 'a school night.' Tons of 'school nights' vs. one Prince. Stupid choice."

Female, 58, Colorado

Coda

Regret and Redemption

When I first reviewed the data from the American Regret Project, I fixated on a pair of findings that annoyed me.

Recall that the prerequisite for experiencing regret is agency—exercising some measure of control over at least some aspects of our lives. I wondered whether the people in my sample felt this sense of dominion over their choices and actions. That is, did they believe they had free will? Or did they instead believe they weren't actually in charge—that their lives unfolded as part of a larger plan and beyond their control?

I posed both questions.

I asked our 4,489 respondents: Do you believe that people have free will—that they largely control their decisions and choices?

A huge majority—82 percent of the population—answered "Yes."

Score one for personal agency.

Elsewhere in the survey, I also asked: Do you believe that most things in life happen for a reason?

A huge majority—78 percent of the population—also answered "Yes."

Score one for fate.

And let's declare the game a tie—as well as a conceptual knot.

When I overlaid the responses to both questions, the results were confounding. Just 5 percent of the sample disagreed with both propositions. Those people said they didn't have free will and that things didn't happen for a reason. Call this tiny cohort the *nihilists*.

Meanwhile, 10 percent believed they exercised free will while rejecting the idea that events unfold for a purpose. Call this group the *individualists*. Another 10 percent held the reverse view. Free will was a myth and everything happened for a reason, they said. These are the *fatalists*.

But the largest group by far—three out of four Americans in the survey—maintained both that they have free will and that most things happen for a reason, two beliefs that seem to contradict each other.

What to call this mystifying group?

I thought about it awhile. And after careful consideration, the name I've chosen to assign them is . . . the *humans*.

Open the hood of regret, and you'll see that the engine powering it is storytelling. Our very ability to experience regret depends on our imagination's capacity to travel backward in time, rewrite events, and fashion a happier ending than in the original draft. Our capacity to respond to regret, to mobilize it for good, depends on our narrative skills—disclosing the tale, analyzing its components, and crafting and recrafting the next chapter.

Regret depends on storytelling. And that raises a question: In these stories, are we the creator or the character, the playwright or the performer?

As the survey respondents told me—with their seemingly contradictory, bafflingly human responses to my perfectly logical questions—we are both. If our lives are the stories we tell ourselves, regret reminds us that we have a dual role. We are both the authors and the actors. We can shape the plot but not fully. We can toss aside the script but not always. We live at the intersection of free will and circumstance.

Dan McAdams is a Northwestern University psychologist who has long argued that people forge their identities through stories. According to his research, two prototypical narratives wrestle for primacy as we make sense of our existence. One is what he calls "contamination sequences"—in which events go from good to bad. The other he calls "redemption sequences"—in which events go from bad to good.[1]

McAdams has found that people whose identities involve contamination narratives tend to be unhappy with their personal lives and unimpressive in their professional contributions. But people with narratives rooted in redemption are the opposite. They are generally more satisfied and accomplished—and they rate their lives as meaningful.

Regret offers us the ultimate redemption narrative. It is as powerful and affirming as any positive emotion. But it arrives on our doorstep wearing a disguise.

Just ask Cheryl Johnson.

The regret she harbored about losing touch with her close friend Jen continued to nag at her—so much so that one morning in May 2021, she pushed past her awkwardness and decided to send Jen an email.

"I suspect it might be strange to hear from me after all these years," the message began.

Although they hadn't communicated in twenty-five years, Jen replied within hours. The two old friends then decided to meet for a virtual lunch to reconnect.

"I finally got to say to her that I knew I made a mistake," Cheryl told me after that lunch, "and how much I regretted losing so many years that could have been spent watching our lives unfold together."

Jen's response?

"But we still have a lot of years left."

If we think about regret like this—looking backward to move forward, seizing what we can control and putting aside what we cannot, crafting our own redemption stories—it can be liberating.

It has been for me.

One of my deeper regrets is that I wasn't kinder to people when I was younger. I'm not sure that happened for a reason, but I am sure I can find reason in the recollection. Now I try (not always successfully) to make kindness a higher priority.

I also regret moments of dishonesty, which were not cataclysmic yet somehow remain seared in my memory. Now I try to avoid placing new items on those mental shelves by working harder to do the right thing.

I regret certain educational and professional choices that I made. But now I kick myself less for these blunders and use the lessons I learned to guide the rest of my life and to inform the advice I offer others.

I regret not forging enough close connections with friends, mentors, and colleagues. Now I try harder to reach out.

I regret not taking enough entrepreneurial and creative risks, not being as bold as my privilege allows and my heart desires. Now . . . stay tuned.

After a few years immersed in the science and experience of our most misunderstood emotion, I've discovered about myself what I've discovered about others. Regret makes me human. Regret makes me better. Regret gives me hope.

Acknowledgments

I sure don't regret having so many amazing people in my corner. Special thanks to:

Jake Morrissey for his wise (and badly needed) structural revisions to the book, for his elegant refinements of my inelegant prose, and for our regular conversations, which were always a bright spot during the dark days of the pandemic.

Team Riverhead—especially Ashley Garland, Lydia Hirt, Geoff Kloske, Jynne Dilling Martin, and Ashley Sutton—for putting their brains and muscle behind all projects Pink.

Rafe Sagalyn, literary agent extraordinaire, for his sage advice on this book and for our twenty-five-year partnership on all books.

The sixteen thousand people who completed the World Regret Survey, the nearly five thousand people whose opinions formed the American Regret Project, and the more than one hundred people who sat for (mostly virtual) interviews about (decidedly real) matters.

Joseph Hinson, Nathan Torrence, and Josh Kennedy, along with the crew at Qualtrics, for building the World Regret Survey and making it powerful and easy to use.

Acknowledgments

Fred Kofman for jump-starting my stalled mental car with a few jolts of purpose.

Cameron French for once again finding facts, fixing fictions, and being a Swiss Army knife of research skills.

Tanya Maiboroda for once again delivering first-class graphics despite coach-class instructions.

Sophia Pink for her next-level quantitative skills and for unearthing shiny nuggets of insight buried in muddy heaps of data.

Eliza Pink and Saul Pink for their eloquent example of how to finish strong—in college and in high school—during suboptimal conditions.

Jessica Lerner for everything.

Notes

Chapter 1: The Life-Thwarting Nonsense of No Regrets

1. This account is based on two Piaf biographies (Burke, Carolyn. *No regrets: The life of Edith Piaf.* London: A&C Black, 2012; Noli, Jean. *Edith Piaf: Trois ans pour mourir.* Pocket Presses, 1978) as well as a 2003 interview with Charles Dumont (Lichfield, John. "Charles Dumont: Regrets? Too few to mention." *The Independent,* October 9, 2003).

2. Heldenfels, Richard. "TV mailbag: What's the song in the Allstate commercial?" *Akron Beacon Journal,* October 8, 2020; Wilder, Ben. "New Allstate commercial—actors, location, and music." *Out of the Wilderness,* December 13, 2020. Available at: https://outofthewilderness.me /2020/11/08/allstate/.

3. Peale, Norman Vincent. "No room for regrets." *Guideposts,* December 10, 2008; Wolf, Richard. "Ruth Bader Ginsburg, in her 'own words.'" *USA Today,* October 3, 2016; Blair, Gwenda. "How Norman Vincent Peale taught Donald Trump to worship himself." *Politico Magazine,* October 6, 2015; Vecsey, George. "Norman Vincent Peale, preacher of gospel optimism, dies at 95." *New York Times,* December 26, 1993; Greenhouse, Linda. "Ruth Bader Ginsburg, Supreme Court's feminist icon, is dead at 87." *New York Times,* September 18, 2020.

4. Chen, Joyce. "Angelina Jolie wrote foreword to ex-husband Billy Bob Thornton's new memoir." *New York Daily News,* February 23, 2012; Robhemed, Natalie. "Laverne Cox on breaking down barriers in Hollywood and beyond." *Forbes,* May 13, 2016; Feloni, Richard. "Tony Robbins reveals what he's learned from financial power players like Carl Icahn and Ray Dalio." *Business Insider,* November 18, 2014; Elliot, Paul. "Slash: A decade of drugs was not money well spent." *Classic Rock,* June 12, 2015. Alas, I could not find the original instances of the Dylan and Travolta quotations, but they are widely cited and, to my knowledge, unrefuted. (See, e.g., https://www .reddit.com/r/quotes/comments/bdtnn5/i_dont_believe_in_regrets_regrets_just_keep_you/.)

5. https://catalog.loc.gov.

6. Liszewski, Walter, Elizabeth Kream, Sarah Helland, Amy Cavigli, Bridget C. Lavin, and Andrea Murina. "The demographics and rates of tattoo complications, regret, and unsafe tattooing practices: A cross-sectional study." *Dermatologic Surgery* 41, no. 11 (2015): 1283–89; Kurniadi, Ivan, Farida Tabri, Asnawi Madjid, Anis Irawan Anwar, and Widya Widita. "Laser tattoo removal: Fundamental principles and practical approach." *Dermatologic Therapy* (2020): e14418; Harris Poll. "Tattoo takeover: Three in ten Americans have tattoos, and most don't stop at just one." February 10, 2016. Available at: https://bit.ly/35UIndU; Leigh, Harri. "Tattoo removal

revenue about to hit record." *Lehigh Valley Public Media*, October 16, 2018; Allied Market Research. "Tattoo removal market size: Industry forecast by 2027." October 2020. Available at: https://www.alliedmarketresearch.com/tattoo-removal-market; Ellison, Katherine. "Getting his tattoo took less than 20 minutes. Regret set in within hours." *Washington Post*, May 31, 2020.

7. Markowitz, Harry. "Portfolio selection." *Journal of Finance* 7 (1952): 77–91; Markowitz, Harry M. "Foundations of portfolio theory." *Journal of Finance* 46, no. 2 (1991): 469–77.

8. Forgeard, M. J. C., and M. E. P. Seligman. "Seeing the glass half full: A review of the causes and consequences of optimism." *Pratiques Psychologiques* 18, no. 2 (2012): 107–120; Rasmussen, Heather N., Michael F. Scheier, and Joel B. Greenhouse. "Optimism and physical health: A meta-analytic review." *Annals of Behavioral Medicine* 37, no. 3 (2009): 239–56.

9. Lyubomirsky, Sonja, Laura King, and Ed Diener. "The benefits of frequent positive affect: Does happiness lead to success?" *Psychological Bulletin* 131, no. 6 (2005): 803.

10. See, e.g., Ford, Brett Q., Phoebe Lam, Oliver P. John, and Iris B. Mauss. "The psychological health benefits of accepting negative emotions and thoughts: Laboratory, diary, and longitudinal evidence." *Journal of Personality and Social Psychology* 115, no. 6 (2018): 1075.

Chapter 2: Why Regret Makes Us Human

1. Greenberg, George, and Mary FitzPatrick. "Regret as an essential ingredient in psychotherapy." *The Psychotherapy Patient* 5, no. 1–2 (1989): 35–46.

2. Bell, David E. "Reply: Putting a premium on regret." *Management Science* 31, no. 1 (1985): 117–22.

3. Guthrie, Chris. "Carhart, constitutional rights, and the psychology of regret." *Southern California Law Review* 81 (2007): 877, citing Hampshire, Stuart. "Thought and action." (1959).

4. Guttentag, Robert, and Jennifer Ferrell. "Reality compared with its alternatives: Age differences in judgments of regret and relief." *Developmental Psychology* 40, no. 5 (2004): 764. See also, Uprichard, Brian, and Teresa McCormack. "Becoming kinder: Prosocial choice and the development of interpersonal regret." *Child Development* 90, no. 4 (2019): e486–e504.

5. Gautam, Shalini, Thomas Suddendorf, Julie D. Henry, and Jonathan Redshaw. "A taxonomy of mental time travel and counterfactual thought: Insights from cognitive development." *Behavioural Brain Research* 374 (2019): 112108; Burns, Patrick, Kevin J. Riggs, and Sarah R. Beck. "Executive control and the experience of regret." *Journal of Experimental Child Psychology* 111, no. 3 (2012): 501–15. (This source argues that "the late emergence of regret . . . is a result of the executive demands of simultaneously holding in mind and comparing dual representations of reality.")

6. O'Connor, Eimear, Teresa McCormack, and Aidan Feeney. "The development of regret." *Journal of Experimental Child Psychology* 111, no. 1 (2012): 120–27; McCormack, Teresa, Eimear O'Connor, Sarah Beck, and Aidan Feeney. "The development of regret and relief about the outcomes of risky decisions." *Journal of Experimental Child Psychology* 148 (2016): 1–19; O'Connor, Eimear, Teresa McCormack, Sarah R. Beck, and Aidan Feeney. "Regret and adaptive decision making in young children." *Journal of Experimental Child Psychology* 135 (2015): 86–92.

7. McCormack, Teresa, and Aidan Feeney. "The development of the experience and anticipation of regret." *Cognition and Emotion* 29, no. 2 (2015): 266–80.

8. Rafetseder, Eva, Maria Schwitalla, and Josef Perner. "Counterfactual reasoning: From childhood to adulthood." *Journal of Experimental Child Psychology* 114, no. 3 (2013): 389–404; Guttentag, Robert, and Jennifer Ferrell. "Children's understanding of anticipatory regret and disappointment." *Cognition and Emotion* 22, no. 5 (2008): 815–32; Habib, Marianne, M. Cassotti, G. Borst, G. Simon, A. Pineau, O. Houdé, and S. Moutier. "Counterfactually mediated emotions: A developmental study of regret and relief in a probabilistic gambling task." *Journal of Experimental Child Psychology* 112, no. 2 (2012): 265–74.

9. Camille, Nathalie, Giorgio Coricelli, Jerome Sallet, Pascale Pradat-Diehl, Jean-René Duhamel, and Angela Sirigu. "The involvement of the orbitofrontal cortex in the experience of regret."

Notes

Science 304, no. 5674 (2004): 1167–70. See also, Coricelli, Giorgio, Hugo D. Critchley, Mateus Joffily, John P. O'Doherty, Angela Sirigu, and Raymond J. Dolan. "Regret and its avoidance: A neuroimaging study of choice behavior." *Nature Neuroscience* 8, no. 9 (2005): 1255–62. (This source shows that the same neural circuitry is used for both prospective regret and anticipated regret.); Ursu, Stefan, and Cameron S. Carter. "Outcome representations, counterfactual comparisons and the human orbitofrontal cortex: Implications for neuroimaging studies of decision-making." *Cognitive Brain Research* 23, no. 1 (2005): 51–60.

10. Solca, Federica, Barbara Poletti, Stefano Zago, Chiara Crespi, Francesca Sassone, Annalisa Lafronza, Anna Maria Maraschi, Jenny Sassone, Vincenzo Silani, and Andrea Ciammola. "Counterfactual thinking deficit in Huntington's disease." *PLOS One* 10, no. 6 (2015): e0126773.

11. McNamara, Patrick, Raymon Durso, Ariel Brown, and A. Lynch. "Counterfactual cognitive deficit in persons with Parkinson's disease." *Journal of Neurology, Neurosurgery, and Psychiatry* 74, no. 8 (2003): 1065–70.

12. Contreras, Fernando, Auria Albacete, Pere Castellví, Agnès Caño, Bessy Benejam, and José Manuel Menchón. "Counterfactual reasoning deficits in schizophrenia patients." *PLOS One* 11, no. 2 (2016): e0148440; Hooker, Christine, Neal J. Roese, and Sohee Park. "Impoverished counterfactual thinking is associated with schizophrenia." *Psychiatry* 63, no. 4 (2000): 326–35. (Psychopathic individuals do experience retrospective regret. But they seem unaffected by prospective regret when making decisions); Baskin-Sommers, Arielle, Allison M. Stuppy-Sullivan, and Joshua W. Buckholtz. "Psychopathic individuals exhibit but do not avoid regret during counterfactual decision making." *Proceedings of the National Academy of Sciences* 113, no. 50 (2016): 14438–43.

13. Tagini, Sofia, Federica Solca, Silvia Torre, Agostino Brugnera, Andrea Ciammola, Ketti Mazzocco, Roberta Ferrucci, Vincenzo Silani, Gabriella Pravettoni, and Barbara Poletti. "Counterfactual thinking in psychiatric and neurological diseases: A scoping review." *PLOS One* 16, no. 2 (2021): e0246388.

14. Gilovich, Thomas, and Victoria Husted Medvec. "The temporal pattern to the experience of regret." *Journal of Personality and Social Psychology* 67, no. 3 (1994): 357. See also Zeelenberg, Marcel, and Rik Pieters. "A theory of regret regulation 1.0." *Journal of Consumer Psychology* 17, no. 1 (2007): 3–18. ("All other negative emotions can be experienced without choice, but regret cannot."); Hammell, C., and A. Y. C. Chan. "Improving physical task performance with counterfactual and prefactual thinking." *PLOS One* 11, no. 12 (2016): e0168181. https://doi.org/10.1371/journal.pone.0168181.

15. Landman, Janet. *Regret: The persistence of the possible.* New York: Oxford University Press, 1993, 47.

16. Zeelenberg, Marcel, and Rik Pieters. "A theory of regret regulation 1.0." *Journal of Consumer Psychology* 17, no. 1 (2007): 3–18.

17. Fleming, Eleanor B., Duong Nguyen, Joseph Afful, Margaret D. Carroll, and Phillip D. Woods. "Prevalence of daily flossing among adults by selected risk factors for periodontal disease—United States, 2011–2014." *Journal of Periodontology* 89, no. 8 (2018): 933–39; Sternberg, Steve. "How many Americans floss their teeth?" *U.S. News and World Report*, May 2, 2016.

18. Shimanoff, Susan B. "Commonly named emotions in everyday conversations." *Perceptual and Motor Skills* (1984).

19. Saffrey, Colleen, Amy Summerville, and Neal J. Roese. "Praise for regret: People value regret above other negative emotions." *Motivation and Emotion* 32, no. 1 (2008): 46–54.

20. Bjälkebring, Pär, Daniel Västfjäll, Ola Svenson, and Paul Slovic. "Regulation of experienced and anticipated regret in daily decision making." *Emotion* 16, no. 3 (2016): 381.

21. Morrison, Mike, and Neal J. Roese. "Regrets of the typical American: Findings from a nationally representative sample." *Social Psychological and Personality Science* 2, no. 6 (2011): 576–83.

22. Gilovich, Thomas, and Victoria Husted Medvec. "The experience of regret: What, when, and why." *Psychological Review* 102, no. 2 (1995): 379.

23. Langley, William. "Edith Piaf: Mistress of heartbreak and pain who had a few regrets after all." *The Daily Telegraph*, October 13, 2013.

Chapter 3: At Leasts *and* If Onlys
1. Roese, Neal J., and Kai Epstude. "The functional theory of counterfactual thinking: New evidence, new challenges, new insights." In *Advances in experimental and social psychology*, vol. 56, 1–79. Academic Press, 2017.
2. Medvec, Victoria Husted, Scott F. Madey, and Thomas Gilovich. "When less is more: Counterfactual thinking and satisfaction among Olympic medalists." *Journal of Personality and Social Psychology* 69, no. 4 (1995): 603. (The study also examined medalists in the 1994 Empire State Games.)
3. Maxwell, Scott E., Michael Y. Lau, and George S. Howard. "Is psychology suffering from a replication crisis? What does 'failure to replicate' really mean?" *American Psychologist* 70, no. 6 (2015): 487; Yong, Ed. "Psychology's replication crisis is running out of excuses." *The Atlantic*, November 19, 2018.
4. Matsumoto, David, and Bob Willingham. "The thrill of victory and the agony of defeat: Spontaneous expressions of medal winners of the 2004 Athens Olympic Games." *Journal of Personality and Social Psychology* 91, no. 3 (2006): 568.
5. Hedgcock, William M., Andrea W. Luangrath, and Raelyn Webster. "Counterfactual thinking and facial expressions among Olympic medalists: A conceptual replication of Medvec, Madey, and Gilovich's (1995) findings." *Journal of Experimental Psychology: General* (2020). (Those who outperformed expectations also smiled more. Also, while the replication has been strong, one study has argued that silver medalists have higher expectations than bronze medalists and are therefore more likely to be disappointed.); McGraw, A. Peter, Barbara A. Mellers, and Philip E. Tetlock. "Expectations and emotions of Olympic athletes." *Journal of Experimental Social Psychology* 41, no. 4 (2005): 438–46. (Another found that the expressions of the silver and bronze medalists were similar, but that in interviews the silver medalists expressed more counterfactual thoughts.); Allen, Mark S., Sarah J. Knipler, and Amy Y. C. Chan. "Happiness and counterfactual thinking at the 2016 Summer Olympic Games." *Journal of Sports Sciences* 37, no. 15 (2019): 1762–69.
6. "Emma Johansson tog OS-silver i Rio." *Expressen Sport*, August 7, 2016. Available at: https://www.expressen.se/sport/os-2014/emma-johansson-tog-os-silver-i-rio/.
7. Zeelenberg, Marcel, and Rik Pieters. "A theory of regret regulation 1.0." *Journal of Consumer Psychology* 17, no. 1 (2007): 3–18; Roese, Neal J., and Taekyun Hur. "Affective determinants of counterfactual thinking." *Social Cognition* 15, no. 4 (1997): 274–90; Nasco, Suzanne Altobello, and Kerry L. Marsh. "Gaining control through counterfactual thinking." *Personality and Social Psychology Bulletin* 25, no. 5 (1999): 557–69.
8. Summerville, Amy, and Neal J. Roese. "Dare to compare: Fact-based versus simulation-based comparison in daily life." *Journal of Experimental Social Psychology* 44, no. 3 (2008): 664–71.
9. Teigen, Karl Halvor, and Tine K. Jensen. "Unlucky victims or lucky survivors? Spontaneous counterfactual thinking by families exposed to the tsunami disaster." *European Psychologist* 16, no. 1 (2011): 48.
10. See, e.g., FitzGibbon, Lily, Asuka Komiya, and Kou Murayama. "The lure of counterfactual curiosity: People incur a cost to experience regret." *Psychological Science* 32, no. 2 (2021): 241–55.

Chapter 4: Why Regret Makes Us Better
1. Ku, Gillian. "Learning to de-escalate: The effects of regret in escalation of commitment." *Organizational Behavior and Human Decision Processes* 105, no. 2 (2008): 221–32.

Notes

2. Kray, Laura J., and Michele J. Gelfand. "Relief versus regret: The effect of gender and negotiating norm ambiguity on reactions to having one's first offer accepted." *Social Cognition* 27, no. 3 (2009): 418–36.

3. Galinsky, Adam D., Vanessa L. Seiden, Peter H. Kim, and Victoria Husted Medvec. "The dissatisfaction of having your first offer accepted: The role of counterfactual thinking in negotiations." *Personality and Social Psychology Bulletin* 28, no. 2 (2002): 271–83.

4. Kray, Laura J., Adam D. Galinsky, and Keith D. Markman. "Counterfactual structure and learning from experience in negotiations." *Journal of Experimental Social Psychology* 45, no. 4 (2009): 979–82.

5. Reb, Jochen. "Regret aversion and decision process quality: Effects of regret salience on decision process carefulness." *Organizational Behavior and Human Decision Processes* 105, no. 2 (2008): 169–82. See also, Smallman, Rachel, and Neal J. Roese. "Counterfactual thinking facilitates behavioral intentions." *Journal of Experimental Social Psychology* 45, no. 4 (2009): 845–52.

6. Galinsky, Adam D., and Gordon B. Moskowitz. "Counterfactuals as behavioral primes: Priming the simulation heuristic and consideration of alternatives." *Journal of Experimental Social Psychology* 36, no. 4 (2000): 384–409. See also, Epstude, Kai, and Kai J. Jonas. "Regret and counterfactual thinking in the face of inevitability: The case of HIV-positive men." *Social Psychological and Personality Science* 6, no. 2 (2015): 157–63. (Among HIV-positive men, regret sent well-being down but increased the propensity to practice safe sex.)

7. Meldrum, Helen Mary. "Reflecting or ruminating: Listening to the regrets of life science leaders." *International Journal of Organization Theory and Behavior* (2021).

8. Schwartz, Barry. *The paradox of choice: Why more is less.* New York: Ecco, 2004.

9. O'Connor, Eimear, Teresa McCormack, and Aidan Feeney. "Do children who experience regret make better decisions? A developmental study of the behavioral consequences of regret." *Child Development* 85, no. 5 (2014): 1995–2010.

10. Markman, Keith D., Matthew N. McMullen, and Ronald A. Elizaga. "Counterfactual thinking, persistence, and performance: A test of the Reflection and Evaluation Model." *Journal of Experimental Social Psychology* 44, no. 2 (2008): 421–28. (Certain types of downward counterfactuals also improved performance, though not nearly as much as these evaluative upward counterfactuals.)

11. Roese, Neal J. "The functional basis of counterfactual thinking." *Journal of Personality and Social Psychology* 66, no. 5 (1994): 805.

12. Markman, Keith D., Igor Gavanski, Steven J. Sherman, and Matthew N. McMullen. "The mental simulation of better and worse possible worlds." *Journal of Experimental Social Psychology* 29, no. 1 (1993): 87–109.

13. Galinsky, Adam D., and Gordon B. Moskowitz. "Counterfactuals as behavioral primes: Priming the simulation heuristic and consideration of alternatives." *Journal of Experimental Social Psychology* 36, no. 4 (2000): 384–409. (In this case, it was counterfactual thinking itself, rather than the direction of the counterfactual, that seemed to produce the effect.) See also, Saffrey, Colleen, Amy Summerville, and Neal J. Roese. "Praise for regret: People value regret above other negative emotions." *Motivation and Emotion* 32, no. 1 (2008): 46–54.

14. Gao, Hongmei, Yan Zhang, Fang Wang, Yan Xu, Ying-Yi Hong, and Jiang Jiang. "Regret causes ego-depletion and finding benefits in the regrettable events alleviates ego-depletion." *Journal of General Psychology* 141, no. 3 (2014): 169–206.

15. Wang, Yang, Benjamin F. Jones, and Dashun Wang. "Early-career setback and future career impact." *Nature Communications* 10, no. 1 (2019): 1–10. (A few of the scientists in the narrow miss group apparently left the profession—or at least didn't apply for many subsequent grants. But the researchers concluded that screening out these perhaps less able scientists was not responsible for the difference.)

Notes

16. Kray, Laura J., Linda G. George, Katie A. Liljenquist, Adam D. Galinsky, Philip E. Tetlock, and Neal J. Roese. "From what might have been to what must have been: Counterfactual thinking creates meaning." *Journal of Personality and Social Psychology* 98, no. 1 (2010): 106. See also Choi, Hyeman, and Keith D. Markman. "'If only I had' versus 'If only I had not': Mental deletions, mental additions, and perceptions of meaning in life events." *Journal of Positive Psychology* 14, no. 5 (2019): 672–80. (Subtractive counterfactuals enhance meaning more than additive counterfactuals, which more often serve to prepare for the future.)

17. Roese, Neal J., and Kai Epstude. "The functional theory of counterfactual thinking: New evidence, new challenges, new insights." In *Advances in experimental social psychology*, vol. 56, 1–79. Academic Press, 2017; Heintzelman, Samantha J., Justin Christopher, Jason Trent, and Laura A. King. "Counterfactual thinking about one's birth enhances well-being judgments." *Journal of Positive Psychology* 8, no. 1 (2013): 44–49.

18. Ersner-Hershfield, Hal, Adam D. Galinsky, Laura J. Kray, and Brayden G. King. "Company, country, connections: Counterfactual origins increase organizational commitment, patriotism, and social investment." *Psychological Science* 21, no. 10 (2010): 1479–86.

19. Stewart, Abigail J., and Elizabeth A. Vandewater. "If I had it to do over again . . . Midlife review, midcourse corrections, and women's well-being in midlife." *Journal of Personality and Social Psychology* 76, no. 2 (1999): 270.

20. James, William. *The principles of psychology.* Vols. 1–2. Pantianos Classics, 2021, 432–33.

21. Fiske, Susan T. "Thinking is for doing: Portraits of social cognition from daguerreotype to laserphoto." *Journal of Personality and Social Psychology* 63, no. 6 (1992): 877.

22. Hendel, Hilary Jacobs. "Ignoring your emotions is bad for your health. Here's what to do about it." *Time*, February 27, 2018.

23. For a smart critique of this view, see Lukianoff, Greg, and Jonathan Haidt. *The coddling of the American mind: How good intentions and bad ideas are setting up a generation for failure.* New York: Penguin Books, 2019.

24. Monroe, Michelle Renee, John J. Skowronski, William MacDonald, and Sarah E. Wood. "The mildly depressed experience more post-decisional regret than the non-depressed." *Journal of Social and Clinical Psychology* 24, no. 5 (2005): 665–90; Callander, Gemma, Gary P. Brown, Philip Tata, and Lesley Regan. "Counterfactual thinking and psychological distress following recurrent miscarriage." *Journal of Reproductive and Infant Psychology* 25, no. 1 (2007): 51–65; Gilbar, Ora, Nirit Plivazky, and Sharon Gil. "Counterfactual thinking, coping strategies, and coping resources as predictors of PTSD diagnosed in physically injured victims of terror attacks." *Journal of Loss and Trauma* 15, no. 4 (2010): 304–24.

25. Saffrey, Colleen, Amy Summerville, and Neal J. Roese. "Praise for regret: People value regret above other negative emotions." *Motivation and Emotion* 32, no. 1 (2008): 46–54.

26. Broomhall, Anne Gene, Wendy J. Phillips, Donald W. Hine, and Natasha M. Loi. "Upward counterfactual thinking and depression: A meta-analysis." *Clinical Psychology Review* 55 (2017): 56–73; Roese, Neal J., Kai Epstude, Florian Fessel, Mike Morrison, Rachel Smallman, Amy Summerville, Adam D. Galinsky, and Suzanne Segerstrom. "Repetitive regret, depression, and anxiety: Findings from a nationally representative survey." *Journal of Social and Clinical Psychology* 28, no. 6 (2009): 671–88.

27. Zeelenberg, Marcel, and Rik Pieters. "A theory of regret regulation 1.0." *Journal of Consumer Psychology* 17, no. 1 (2007): 3–18. Zeelenberg and Pieters argue that "feeling is for doing," noting that negative affect is a "signal to the organism that corrective action and thinking are required."

28. Crum, Alia J., Peter Salovey, and Shawn Achor. "Rethinking stress: The role of mindsets in determining the stress response." *Journal of Personality and Social Psychology* 104, no. 4 (2013): 716.

Notes

29. Ford, Brett Q., Phoebe Lam, Oliver P. John, and Iris B. Mauss. "The psychological health benefits of accepting negative emotions and thoughts: Laboratory, diary, and longitudinal evidence." *Journal of Personality and Social Psychology* 115, no. 6 (2018): 1075.
30. Kray, Laura J., Linda G. George, Katie A. Liljenquist, Adam D. Galinsky, Philip E. Tetlock, and Neal J. Roese. "From what might have been to what must have been: Counterfactual thinking creates meaning." *Journal of Personality and Social Psychology* 98, no. 1 (2010): 106.
31. Lippke, Andrea Codrington. "In make-do objects, collectors find beauty beyond repair." *New York Times*, December 15, 2010.

Chapter 5: Regret on the Surface

1. U.S. Department of Commerce, Bureau of the Census, Current Population Reports (Series P-20, No. 45), October 22, 1953. Table 11.
2. Erskine, Hazel. "The polls: Hopes, fears, and regrets." *Public Opinion Quarterly* 37, no. 1 (1973): 132–45.
3. Landman, Janet, and Jean D. Manis. "What might have been: Counterfactual thought concerning personal decisions." *British Journal of Psychology* 83, no. 4 (1992): 473–77.
4. Metha, Arlene T., Richard T. Kinnier, and Ellen H. McWhirter. "A pilot study on the regrets and priorities of women." *Psychology of Women Quarterly* 13, no. 2 (1989): 167–74.
5. Lecci, Len, Morris A. Okun, and Paul Karoly. "Life regrets and current goals as predictors of psychological adjustment." *Journal of Personality and Social Psychology* 66, no. 4 (1994): 731.
6. DeGenova, Mary Kay. "If you had your life to live over again: What would you do differently?" *International Journal of Aging and Human Development* 34, no. 2 (1992): 135–43.
7. Gilovich, Thomas, and Victoria Husted Medvec. "The temporal pattern to the experience of regret." *Journal of Personality and Social Psychology* 67, no. 3 (1994): 357.
8. Hattiangadi, Nina, Victoria Husted Medvec, and Thomas Gilovich. "Failing to act: Regrets of Terman's geniuses." *International Journal of Aging and Human Development* 40, no. 3 (1995): 175–85. (These men and women were the so-called "Termites"—the child geniuses Lewis Terman began studying in the 1920s and whose life paths he and colleagues continued to chart throughout their lives.)
9. Roese, Neal J., and Amy Summerville. "What we regret most . . . and why." *Personality and Social Psychology Bulletin* 31, no. 9 (2005): 1273–85.
10. Morrison, Mike, and Neal J. Roese. "Regrets of the typical American: Findings from a nationally representative sample." *Social Psychological and Personality Science* 2, no. 6 (2011): 576–83.

Chapter 6: The Four Core Regrets

1. Chomsky, Noam. *Syntactic structures.* New York: De Gruyter Mouton, 2009; Chomsky, Noam. *Deep structure, surface structure and semantic interpretation.* New York: De Gruyter Mouton, 2019; Anderson, Stephen R. "On the role of deep structure in semantic interpretation." *Foundations of Language* (1971): 387–96.
2. Chomsky, Noam. *Aspects of the theory of syntax.* Cambridge, MA: MIT Press, 1965.

Chapter 7: Foundation Regrets

1. O'Donoghue, Ted, and Matthew Rabin. "Doing it now or later." *American Economic Review* 89, no. 1 (1999): 103–124; Frederick, Shane, George Loewenstein, and Ted O'Donoghue. "Time discounting and time preference: A critical review." *Journal of Economic Literature* 40, no. 2 (2002): 351–401.
2. Robbins, Jamie E., Leilani Madrigal, and Christopher T. Stanley. "Retrospective remorse: College athletes' reported regrets from a single season." *Journal of Sport Behavior* 38, no. 2 (2015).
3. Hemingway, Ernest. *The sun also rises.* New York: Scribner, 1954.

Notes

4. Wagenaar, William A., and Sabato D. Sagaria. "Misperception of exponential growth." *Perception and Psychophysics* 18, no. 6 (1975): 416–22; Levy, Matthew, and Joshua Tasoff. "Exponential-growth bias and lifecycle consumption." *Journal of the European Economic Association* 14, no. 3 (2016): 545–83.

5. Jones, Edward E., and Victor A. Harris. "The attribution of attitudes." *Journal of Experimental Social Psychology* 3, no. 1 (1967): 1–24; Kelley, Harold H. "The processes of causal attribution." *American Psychologist* 28, no. 2 (1973): 107; Bem, Daryl J. "Self-perception theory." In *Advances in experimental social psychology*, vol. 6, 1–62. Academic Press, 1972; Ross, Lee. "The intuitive psychologist and his shortcomings: Distortions in the attribution process." In *Advances in experimental social psychology*, vol. 10, 173–220. Academic Press, 1977; Henrich, Joseph, Steven J. Heine, and Ara Norenzayan. "The weirdest people in the world?" *Behavioral and Brain Sciences* 33, no. 2–3 (2010): 61–83.

Chapter 8: Boldness Regrets

1. Costa, Paul T., and Robert R. McCrae. "Revised NEO personality inventory (NEO-PI-R) and NEO five-factor inventory (NEO-FFI)." *Psychological Assessment Resources* (1992); Ones, Deniz S., and Stephan Dilchert. "How special are executives? How special should executive selection be? Observations and recommendations." *Industrial and Organizational Psychology* 2, no. 2 (2009): 163–70.

2. Margolis, Seth, and Sonja Lyubomirsky. "Experimental manipulation of extraverted and introverted behavior and its effects on well-being." *Journal of Experimental Psychology: General* 149, no. 4 (2020): 719. See also Kuijpers, E., J. Pickett, B. Wille, and J. Hofmans. "Do you feel better when you behave more extraverted than you are? The relationship between cumulative counterdispositional extraversion and positive feelings." *Personality and Social Psychology Bulletin* (2021): 01461672211015062.

3. Gilovich, Thomas, and Victoria Husted Medvec. "The temporal pattern to the experience of regret." *Journal of personality and social psychology* 67, no. 3 (1994): 357; Gilovich, Thomas, and Victoria Husted Medvec. "The experience of regret: What, when, and why." *Psychological review* 102, no. 2 (1995): 379.

4. Gilovich, Thomas, Ranxiao Frances Wang, Dennis Regan, and Sadafumi Nishina. "Regrets of action and inaction across cultures." *Journal of Cross-Cultural Psychology* 34, no. 1 (2003): 61–71. See also Chen, Jing, Chi-Yue Chiu, Neal J. Roese, Kim-Pong Tam, and Ivy Yee-Man Lau. "Culture and counterfactuals: On the importance of life domains." *Journal of Cross-Cultural Psychology* 37, no. 1 (2006): 75–84.

5. Gilovich, Thomas, and Victoria Husted Medvec. "The temporal pattern to the experience of regret." *Journal of personality and social psychology* 67, no. 3 (1994): 357; Gilovich, Thomas, and Victoria Husted Medvec. "The experience of regret: What, when, and why." *Psychological review* 102, no. 2 (1995): 379; See also Savitsky, Kenneth, Victoria Husted Medvec, and Thomas Gilovich. "Remembering and regretting: The Zeigarnik effect and the cognitive availability of regrettable actions and inactions." *Personality and Social Psychology Bulletin* 23, no. 3 (1997): 248–57.

6. Nash, O. *The Best of Ogden Nash*. Chicago: Ivan R. Dee, 2007.

Chapter 9: Moral Regrets

1. Haidt, Jonathan. *The righteous mind: Why good people are divided by politics and religion*. New York: Vintage, 2012. (I also recommend Haidt's other books: Lukianoff, Greg, and Jonathan Haidt. *The coddling of the American mind: How good intentions and bad ideas are setting up a generation for failure*. New York: Penguin Books, 2019; Haidt, Jonathan. *The happiness hypothesis: Finding modern truth in ancient wisdom*. New York: Basic Books, 2006.)

Notes

2. Haidt, Jonathan. "The emotional dog and its rational tail: A social intuitionist approach to moral judgment." *Psychological Review* 108, no. 4 (2001): 814; Haidt, Jonathan, Fredrik Bjork-lund, and Scott Murphy. "Moral dumbfounding: When intuition finds no reason." Unpublished manuscript, University of Virginia (2000): 191–221.

3. Graham, Jesse, Jonathan Haidt, and Brian A. Nosek. "Liberals and conservatives rely on different sets of moral foundations." *Journal of Personality and Social Psychology* 96, no. 5 (2009): 1029.

4. Graham, Jesse, Jonathan Haidt, Sena Koleva, Matt Motyl, Ravi Iyer, Sean P. Wojcik, and Peter H. Ditto. "Moral foundations theory: The pragmatic validity of moral pluralism." In *Advances in experimental social psychology*, vol. 47, 55–130. Academic Press, 2013.

5. Graham, Jesse, Jonathan Haidt, Sena Koleva, Matt Motyl, Ravi Iyer, Sean P. Wojcik, and Peter H. Ditto. "Moral foundations theory: The pragmatic validity of moral pluralism." In *Advances in experimental social psychology*, vol. 47, 55–130. Academic Press, 2013.

6. Graham, Jesse, Jonathan Haidt, Matt Motyl, Peter Meindl, Carol Iskiwitch, and Marlon Mooij-man. "Moral foundations theory." *Atlas of moral psychology* (2018): 211–22.

7. Lynd, Robert Staughton, and Helen Merrell Lynd. *Middletown: A study in contemporary American culture.* New York: Harcourt, Brace, and Company, 1929.

8. Haidt, Jonathan. *The righteous mind: Why good people are divided by politics and religion.* New York: Vintage, 2012, 163.

9. "Americans' Abortion Views Steady in Past Year." https://news.gallup.com/poll/313094/americans -abortion-views-steady-past-year.aspx.

10. Durkheim, Emile. *The elementary forms of the religious life.* [1912]. New York: Free Press, 1965, 34.

Chapter 10: Connection Regrets

1. The organization was technically a "women's fraternity," because it was not the sister organization of a men's fraternity as most sororities are. But it looked like a sorority and functioned like one, so I'm using that term.

2. Morrison, Mike, Kai Epstude, and Neal J. Roese. "Life regrets and the need to belong." *Social Psychological and Personality Science* 3, no. 6 (2012): 675–81.

3. See, e.g., Eyal, Tal, Mary Steffel, and Nicholas Epley. "Perspective mistaking: Accurately understanding the mind of another requires getting perspective, not taking perspective." *Journal of Personality and Social Psychology* 114, no. 4 (2018): 547.

4. Epley, Nicholas, and Juliana Schroeder. "Mistakenly seeking solitude." *Journal of Experimental Psychology: General* 143, no. 5 (2014): 1980.

5. Boothby, Erica J., and Vanessa K. Bohns. "Why a simple act of kindness is not as simple as it seems: Underestimating the positive impact of our compliments on others." *Personality and Social Psychology Bulletin* (2020): 0146167220949003.

6. Miller, Dale T., and Cathy McFarland. "Pluralistic ignorance: When similarity is interpreted as dissimilarity." *Journal of Personality and Social Psychology* 53, no. 2 (1987): 298; Prentice, Deborah A., and Dale T. Miller. "Pluralistic ignorance and the perpetuation of social norms by unwitting actors." In *Advances in experimental social psychology*, vol. 28, 161–209. Academic Press, 1996; Prentice, Deborah A., and Dale T. Miller. "Pluralistic ignorance and alcohol use on campus: Some consequences of misperceiving the social norm." *Journal of Personality and Social Psychology* 64, no. 2 (1993): 243.

7. Mineo, Liz. "Good genes are nice, but joy is better." *Harvard Gazette* 11 (2017).

8. Mineo, Liz. "Good genes are nice, but joy is better." *Harvard Gazette* 11 (2017).

9. Other research puts this figure higher, though it is still a small minority of parents around the world. See, e.g., Piotrowski, Konrad. "How many parents regret having children and how it is

linked to their personality and health: Two studies with national samples in Poland." *PLOS One* 16, no. 7 (2021): e0254163.

10. Ko, Ahra, Cari M. Pick, Jung Yul Kwon, Michael Barlev, Jaimie Arona Krems, Michael EW Varnum, Rebecca Neel, et al. "Family matters: Rethinking the psychology of human social motivation." *Perspectives on Psychological Science* 15, no. 1 (2020): 173–201.

11. Vaillant, George E. "Happiness is love: Full stop." Unpublished manuscript (2012).

Chapter 11: Opportunity and Obligation

1. Higgins, E. Tory. "Self-discrepancy: A theory relating self and affect." *Psychological Review* 94, no. 3 (1987): 319.

2. Davidai, Shai, and Thomas Gilovich. "The ideal road not taken: The self-discrepancies involved in people's most enduring regrets." *Emotion* 18, no. 3 (2018): 439. (They also suggest that our ideal selves are less attainable, involve abstract values more than concrete actions, and are less dependent on context than our ought selves.)

3. See, e.g., Joel, Samantha, Jason E. Plaks, and Geoff MacDonald. "Nothing ventured, nothing gained: People anticipate more regret from missed romantic opportunities than from rejection." *Journal of Social and Personal Relationships* 36, no. 1 (2019): 305–36.

4. Roese, Neal J., and Amy Summerville. "What we regret most . . . and why." *Personality and Social Psychology Bulletin* 31, no. 9 (2005): 1273–85.

5. This becomes clearer when we examine differences in regret between North American and Asian cultures. While those differences are not vast, people in places like Japan and Korea are more likely to express interpersonal regrets, while North Americans are more likely to express self-oriented regrets. See Komiya, Asuka, Yuri Miyamoto, Motoki Watabe, and Takashi Kusumi. "Cultural grounding of regret: Regret in self and interpersonal contexts." *Cognition and Emotion* 25, no. 6 (2011): 1121–30; Hur, Taekyun, Neal J. Roese, and Jae-Eun Namkoong. "Regrets in the East and West: Role of intrapersonal versus interpersonal norms." *Asian Journal of Social Psychology* 12, no. 2 (2009): 151–56; Komiya, Asuka, Shigehiro Oishi, and Minha Lee. "The rural-urban difference in interpersonal regret." *Personality and Social Psychology Bulletin* 42, no. 4 (2016): 513–25.

Chapter 12: Undoing and At Leasting

1. Zeelenberg, Marcel, Joop van der Pligt, and Antony S. R. Manstead. "Undoing regret on Dutch television: Apologizing for interpersonal regrets involving actions or inactions." *Personality and Social Psychology Bulletin* 24, no. 10 (1998): 1113–19.

2. Goffman, Erving. *Relations in public*. New Brunswick, NJ: Transaction Publishers, 2009, 114.

3. Emmerling, Johannes, and Salmai Qari. "Car ownership and hedonic adaptation." *Journal of Economic Psychology* 61 (2017): 29–38.

4. See, e.g., Gilbert, D. T., E. C. Pinel, T. D. Wilson, S. J. Blumberg, and T. P. Wheatley. "Immune neglect: A source of durability bias in affective forecasting." *Journal of Personality and Social Psychology* 75, no. 3 (1998): 617.

Chapter 13: Disclosure, Compassion, and Distance

1. Deaner, Robert O., Amit V. Khera, and Michael L. Platt. "Monkeys pay per view: Adaptive valuation of social images by rhesus macaques." *Current Biology* 15, no. 6 (2005): 543–48.

2. Tamir, Diana I., and Jason P. Mitchell. "Disclosing information about the self is intrinsically rewarding." *Proceedings of the National Academy of Sciences* 109, no. 21 (2012): 8038–43.

3. Tamir, Diana I., and Jason P. Mitchell. "Disclosing information about the self is intrinsically rewarding." *Proceedings of the National Academy of Sciences* 109, no. 21 (2012): 8038–43.

Notes

4. Frattaroli, Joanne. "Experimental disclosure and its moderators: A meta-analysis." *Psychological Bulletin* 132, no. 6 (2006): 823.

5. Tamir, Diana I., and Jason P. Mitchell. "Disclosing information about the self is intrinsically rewarding." *Proceedings of the National Academy of Sciences* 109, no. 21 (2012): 8038–43.

6. Lyubomirsky, Sonja, Lorie Sousa, and Rene Dickerhoof. "The costs and benefits of writing, talking, and thinking about life's triumphs and defeats." *Journal of Personality and Social Psychology* 90, no. 4 (2006): 692.

7. See, Torre, Jared B., and Matthew D. Lieberman. "Putting feelings into words: Affect labeling as implicit emotion regulation." *Emotion Review* 10, no. 2 (2018): 116–24.

8. Lyubomirsky, Sonja, Lorie Sousa, and Rene Dickerhoof. "The costs and benefits of writing, talking, and thinking about life's triumphs and defeats." *Journal of Personality and Social Psychology* 90, no. 4 (2006): 692. (Emphasis added.)

9. Collins, Nancy L., and Lynn Carol Miller. "Self-disclosure and liking: A meta-analytic review." *Psychological Bulletin* 116, no. 3 (1994): 457. (Emphasis added.)

10. Pennebaker, James W. "Putting stress into words: Health, linguistic, and therapeutic implications." *Behaviour Research and Therapy* 31, no. 6 (1993): 539–48; Pennebaker, James W., and Cindy K. Chung. "Expressive writing, emotional upheavals, and health." In Friedman, Howard S., and Roxane Cohen Silver, eds. *Foundations of health psychology.* New York: Oxford University Press, 2007; Pennebaker, James W. "Writing about emotional experiences as a therapeutic process." *Psychological Science* 8, no. 3 (1997): 162–66; Gortner, Eva-Maria, Stephanie S. Rude, and James W. Pennebaker. "Benefits of expressive writing in lowering rumination and depressive symptoms." *Behavior Therapy* 37, no. 3 (2006): 292–303.

11. Pennebaker, James W. "Writing about emotional experiences as a therapeutic process." *Psychological Science* 8, no. 3 (1997): 162–66.

12. Killham, Margo E., Amber D. Mosewich, Diane E. Mack, Katie E. Gunnell, and Leah J. Ferguson. "Women athletes' self-compassion, self-criticism, and perceived sport performance." *Sport, Exercise, and Performance Psychology* 7, no. 3 (2018): 297; Powers, Theodore A., Richard Koestner, David C. Zuroff, Marina Milyavskaya, and Amy A. Gorin. "The effects of self-criticism and self-oriented perfectionism on goal pursuit." *Personality and Social Psychology Bulletin* 37, no. 7 (2011): 964–75; Powers, Theodore A., Richard Koestner, and David C. Zuroff. "Self-criticism, goal motivation, and goal progress." *Journal of Social and Clinical Psychology* 26, no. 7 (2007): 826–40; Kamen, Leslie P., and Martin E. P. Seligman. "Explanatory style and health." *Current Psychology* 6, no. 3 (1987): 207–18; Buchanan, Gregory McClell, Martin E. P. Seligman, and Martin Seligman, eds. *Explanatory style.* New York: Routledge, 2013.

13. Baumeister, Roy F., Jennifer D. Campbell, Joachim I. Krueger, and Kathleen D. Vohs. "Does high self-esteem cause better performance, interpersonal success, happiness, or healthier lifestyles?" *Psychological Science in the Public Interest* 4, no. 1 (2003): 1–44.

14. Baumeister, Roy F., Laura Smart, and Joseph M. Boden. "Relation of threatened egotism to violence and aggression: The dark side of high self-esteem." *Psychological Review* 103, no. 1 (1996): 5; Raskin, Robert, Jill Novacek, and Robert Hogan. "Narcissism, self-esteem, and defensive self-enhancement." *Journal of Personality* 59, no. 1 (1991): 19–38; Campbell, W. Keith, Eric A. Rudich, and Constantine Sedikides. "Narcissism, self-esteem, and the positivity of self-views: Two portraits of self-love." *Personality and Social Psychology Bulletin* 28, no. 3 (2002): 358–68; Aberson, Christopher L., Michael Healy, and Victoria Romero. "Ingroup bias and self-esteem: A meta-analysis." *Personality and Social Psychology Review* 4, no. 2 (2000): 157–73.

15. Neff, Kristin D., Kristin L. Kirkpatrick, and Stephanie S. Rude. "Self-compassion and adaptive psychological functioning." *Journal of Research in Personality* 41, no. 1 (2007): 139–54.

16. Ferrari, Madeleine, Caroline Hunt, Ashish Harrysunker, Maree J. Abbott, Alissa P. Beath, and Danielle A. Einstein. "Self-compassion interventions and psychosocial outcomes: A

Notes

meta-analysis of RCTs." *Mindfulness* 10, no. 8 (2019): 1455–73; Neff, Kristin D., and Christopher K. Germer. "A pilot study and randomized controlled trial of the mindful self-compassion program." *Journal of Clinical Psychology* 69, no. 1 (2013): 28–44.

17. Neff, Kristin D., Stephanie S. Rude, and Kristin L. Kirkpatrick. "An examination of self-compassion in relation to positive psychological functioning and personality traits." *Journal of Research in Personality* 41, no. 4 (2007): 908–16.

18. Neff, Kristin D., and Christopher K. Germer. "A pilot study and randomized controlled trial of the mindful self-compassion program." *Journal of Clinical Psychology* 69, no. 1 (2013): 28–44.

19. Mahmoud, Mohebi, and Zarei Sahar. "The relationship between mental toughness and self-compassion in elite and non-elite adolescent taekwondo athletes." *Journal of Motor and Behavioral Sciences* 2, no. 1 (2019): 21–31.

20. Neff, Kristin D. "Self-compassion, self-esteem, and well-being." *Social and Personality Psychology Compass* 5, no. 1 (2011): 1–12.

21. Greenberg, Jonathan, Tanya Datta, Benjamin G. Shapero, Gunes Sevinc, David Mischoulon, and Sara W. Lazar. "Compassionate hearts protect against wandering minds: Self-compassion moderates the effect of mind-wandering on depression." *Spirituality in Clinical Practice* 5, no. 3 (2018): 155.

22. Neff, Kristin D., Ya-Ping Hsieh, and Kullaya Dejitterat. "Self-compassion, achievement goals, and coping with academic failure." *Self and Identity* 4, no. 3 (2005): 263–87.

23. Zessin, Ulli, Oliver Dickhäuser, and Sven Garbade. "The relationship between self-compassion and well-being: A meta-analysis." *Applied Psychology: Health and Well-Being* 7, no. 3 (2015): 340–64.

24. Winders, Sarah-Jane, Orlagh Murphy, Kathy Looney, and Gary O'Reilly. "Self-compassion, trauma, and posttraumatic stress disorder: A systematic review." *Clinical Psychology and Psychotherapy* 27, no. 3 (2020): 300–329; Hiraoka, Regina, Eric C. Meyer, Nathan A. Kimbrel, Bryann B. DeBeer, Suzy Bird Gulliver, and Sandra B. Morissette. "Self-compassion as a prospective predictor of PTSD symptom severity among trauma-exposed US Iraq and Afghanistan war veterans." *Journal of Traumatic Stress* 28, no. 2 (2015): 127–33.

25. Phillips, Wendy J., and Donald W. Hine. "Self-compassion, physical health, and health behaviour: A meta-analysis." *Health Psychology Review* 15, no. 1 (2021): 113–39.

26. Zhang, Jia Wei, and Serena Chen. "Self-compassion promotes personal improvement from regret experiences via acceptance." *Personality and Social Psychology Bulletin* 42, no. 2 (2016): 244–58.

27. See, e.g., Breines, Juliana G., and Serena Chen. "Self-compassion increases self-improvement motivation." *Personality and Social Psychology Bulletin* 38, no. 9 (2012): 1133–43.

28. Neff, Kristin D. "Self-compassion, self-esteem, and well-being." *Social and Personality Psychology Compass* 5, no. 1 (2011): 1–12.

29. Kross, Ethan, and Özlem Ayduk. "Making meaning out of negative experiences by self-distancing." *Current Directions in Psychological Science* 20, no. 3 (2011): 187–91.

30. Kross, Ethan, Özlem Ayduk, and Walter Mischel. "When asking 'why' does not hurt distinguishing rumination from reflective processing of negative emotions." *Psychological Science* 16, no. 9 (2005): 709–15.

31. Kross, Ethan, and Özlem Ayduk. "Self-distancing: Theory, research, and current directions." In *Advances in experimental social psychology*, vol. 55, 81–136. Academic Press, 2017.

32. Grossmann, Igor, Anna Dorfman, Harrison Oakes, Henri C. Santos, Kathleen D. Vohs, and Abigail A. Scholer. "Training for wisdom: The distanced-self-reflection diary method." *Psychological Science* 32, no. 3 (2021): 381–94.

33. Ayduk, Özlem, and Ethan Kross. "Enhancing the pace of recovery: Self-distanced analysis of negative experiences reduces blood pressure reactivity." *Psychological Science* 19, no. 3 (2008): 229–31.

Notes

34. Grossmann, Igor, and Ethan Kross. "Exploring Solomon's paradox: Self-distancing eliminates the self-other asymmetry in wise reasoning about close relationships in younger and older adults." *Psychological Science* 25, no. 8 (2014): 1571–80.

35. Leitner, Jordan B., Özlem Ayduk, Rodolfo Mendoza-Denton, Adam Magerman, Rachel Amey, Ethan Kross, and Chad E. Forbes. "Self-distancing improves interpersonal perceptions and behavior by decreasing medial prefrontal cortex activity during the provision of criticism." *Social Cognitive and Affective Neuroscience* 12, no. 4 (2017): 534–43. See also Waytz, Adam, Hal E. Hershfield, and Diana I. Tamir. "Mental simulation and meaning in life." *Journal of Personality and Social Psychology* 108, no. 2 (2015): 336.

36. Thomas, Manoj, and Claire I. Tsai. "Psychological distance and subjective experience: How distancing reduces the feeling of difficulty." *Journal of Consumer Research* 39, no. 2 (2012): 324–40.

37. Kross, Ethan, and Özlem Ayduk. "Self-distancing: Theory, research, and current directions." In *Advances in experimental social psychology*, vol. 55, 81–136. Academic Press, 2017.

38. Bruehlman-Senecal, Emma, and Özlem Ayduk. "This too shall pass: Temporal distance and the regulation of emotional distress." *Journal of Personality and Social Psychology* 108, no. 2 (2015): 356.

39. Rim, SoYon, and Amy Summerville. "How far to the road not taken? The effect of psychological distance on counterfactual direction." *Personality and Social Psychology Bulletin* 40, no. 3 (2014): 391–401.

40. Kross, Ethan, and Özlem Ayduk. "Self-distancing: Theory, research, and current directions." In *Advances in experimental social psychology*, vol. 55, 81–136. Academic Press, 2017.

41. Grossmann, Igor, Anna Dorfman, Harrison Oakes, Henri C. Santos, Kathleen D. Vohs, and Abigail A. Scholer. "Training for wisdom: The distanced-self-reflection diary method." *Psychological Science* 32, no. 3 (2021): 381–94. See also, Kross, Ethan, Emma Bruehlman-Senecal, Jiyoung Park, Aleah Burson, Adrienne Dougherty, Holly Shablack, Ryan Bremner, Jason Moser, and Özlem Ayduk. "Self-talk as a regulatory mechanism: How you do it matters." *Journal of Personality and Social Psychology* 106, no. 2 (2014): 304.

42. Dolcos, Sanda, and Dolores Albarracín. "The inner speech of behavioral regulation: Intentions and task performance strengthen when you talk to yourself as a You." *European Journal of Social Psychology* 44, no. 6 (2014): 636–42.

43. Orvell, Ariana, Ethan Kross, and Susan A. Gelman. "How 'you' makes meaning." *Science* 355, no. 6331 (2017): 1299–1302.

44. Kross, Ethan, Brian D. Vickers, Ariana Orvell, Izzy Gainsburg, Tim P. Moran, Margaret Boyer, John Jonides, Jason Moser, and Özlem Ayduk. "Third-person self-talk reduces Ebola worry and risk perception by enhancing rational thinking." *Applied Psychology: Health and Well-Being* 9, no. 3 (2017): 387–409.

45. Moser, Jason S., Adrienne Dougherty, Whitney I. Mattson, Benjamin Katz, Tim P. Moran, Darwin Guevarra, Holly Shablack, et al. "Third-person self-talk facilitates emotion regulation without engaging cognitive control: Converging evidence from ERP and fMRI." *Scientific Reports* 7, no. 1 (2017): 1–9.

46. This example comes from one of my favorite business books: Heath, Chip, and Dan Heath. *Decisive: How to make better choices in life and work*. New York: Random House, 2013.

47. Koo, Minkyung, Sara B. Algoe, Timothy D. Wilson, and Daniel T. Gilbert. "It's a wonderful life: Mentally subtracting positive events improves people's affective states, contrary to their affective forecasts." *Journal of Personality and Social Psychology* 95, no. 5 (2008): 1217.

Chapter 14: Anticipating Regret

1. The full details of the story, as well as Nobel's deepest motivations, are murky. And some of the particulars do not hold together. See Lenon, Troy. "Swedish inventor Alfred Nobel was

Notes

spurred by his obituary to create the Nobel Prize." *Daily Telegraph*, April 12, 2018; Andrews, Evan. "Did a premature obituary inspire the Nobel Prize?" History.com, July 23, 2020. Available at: https://www.history.com/news/did-a-premature-obituary-inspire-the-nobel-prize. Yet the tale has been told and retold many times, including in the acceptance speeches of Nobel laureates. See, e.g., Gore, Al. "The Nobel lecture given by the Nobel Peace Prize laureate 2007, Al Gore (Oslo, December 10, 2007)." The Nobel Foundation, Oslo (2007).

2. Chapman, Joyce. "Leveraging regret: Maximizing survey participation at the Duke University Libraries." Ithaka S+R blog, May 23, 2017. Available at: https://sr.ithaka.org/blog/leveraging-regret-maximizing-survey-participation-at-the-duke-university-libraries/.

3. See, e.g., Haisley, Emily, Kevin G. Volpp, Thomas Pellathy, and George Loewenstein. "The impact of alternative incentive schemes on completion of health risk assessments." *American Journal of Health Promotion* 26, no. 3 (2012): 184–88; Zeelenberg, Marcel, and Rik Pieters. "Consequences of regret aversion in real life: The case of the Dutch postcode lottery." *Organizational Behavior and Human Decision Processes* 93, no. 2 (2004): 155–68. But they are not always effective. See, e.g., Gandhi, Linnea, Katherine L. Milkman, Sean Ellis, Heather Graci, Dena Gromet, Rayyan Mobarak, Alison Buttenheim, et al. "An experiment evaluating the impact of large-scale, high-payoff vaccine regret lotteries." *High-Payoff Vaccine Regret Lotteries (August 13, 2021)* (2021). (A regret lottery in Philadelphia had barely a negligible effect on increasing COVID vaccinations.)

4. Tversky, Amos, and Daniel Kahneman. "Advances in prospect theory: Cumulative representation of uncertainty." *Journal of Risk and Uncertainty* 5, no. 4 (1992): 297–323.

5. Ravert, Russell D., Linda Y. Fu, and Gregory D. Zimet. "Young adults' COVID-19 testing intentions: The role of health beliefs and anticipated regret." *Journal of Adolescent Health* 68, no. 3 (2021): 460–63.

6. Wolff, Katharina. "COVID-19 vaccination intentions: The theory of planned behavior, optimistic bias, and anticipated regret." *Frontiers in Psychology* 12 (2021).

7. Brewer, Noel T., Jessica T. DeFrank, and Melissa B. Gilkey. "Anticipated regret and health behavior: A meta-analysis." *Health Psychology* 35, no. 11 (2016): 1264.

8. Abraham, Charles, and Paschal Sheeran. "Deciding to exercise: The role of anticipated regret." *British Journal of Health Psychology* 9, no. 2 (2004): 269–78.

9. Steptoe, Andrew, Linda Perkins-Porras, Elisabeth Rink, Sean Hilton, and Francesco P. Cappuccio. "Psychological and social predictors of changes in fruit and vegetable consumption over 12 months following behavioral and nutrition education counseling." *Health Psychology* 23, no. 6 (2004): 574.

10. Penţa, Marcela A., Irina Catrinel Crăciun, and Adriana Băban. "The power of anticipated regret: Predictors of HPV vaccination and seasonal influenza vaccination acceptability among young Romanians." *Vaccine* 38, no. 6 (2020): 1572–78.

11. Chapman, Gretchen B., and Elliot J. Coups. "Emotions and preventive health behavior: Worry, regret, and influenza vaccination." *Health Psychology* 25, no. 1 (2006): 82.

12. Richard, Rene, Nanne K. de Vries, and Joop van der Pligt. "Anticipated regret and precautionary sexual behavior." *Journal of Applied Social Psychology* 28, no. 15 (1998): 1411–28.

13. Ahn, Jisoo, and Lee Ann Kahlor. "No regrets when it comes to your health: Anticipated regret, subjective norms, information insufficiency, and intent to seek health information from multiple sources." *Health Communication* 35, no. 10 (2020): 1295–1302.

14. de Nooijer, Jascha, Lilian Lechner, Math Candel, and Hein de Vries. "Short- and long-term effects of tailored information versus general information on determinants and intentions related to early detection of cancer." *Preventive Medicine* 38, no. 6 (2004): 694–703.

15. Elliott, Mark A., and James A. Thomson. "The social cognitive determinants of offending drivers' speeding behaviour." *Accident Analysis and Prevention* 42, no. 6 (2010): 1595–1605.

Notes

16. Sandberg, Tracy, and Mark Conner. "A mere measurement effect for anticipated regret: Impacts on cervical screening attendance." *British Journal of Social Psychology* 48, no. 2 (2009): 221–36.

17. Conner, Mark, Tracy Sandberg, Brian McMillan, and Andrea Higgins. "Role of anticipated regret, intentions, and intention stability in adolescent smoking initiation." *British Journal of Health Psychology* 11, no. 1 (2006): 85–101.

18. Carfora, Valentina, Daniela Caso, and Mark Conner. "Randomised controlled trial of a text messaging intervention for reducing processed meat consumption: The mediating roles of anticipated regret and intention." *Appetite* 117 (2017): 152–60.

19. Kaiser, Florian G. "A moral extension of the theory of planned behavior: Norms and anticipated feelings of regret in conservationism." *Personality and Individual Differences* 41, no. 1 (2006): 71–81.

20. Mayes, Liz. "At this workshop, writing your own obit means analyzing your past—or future." *Washington Post*, December 10, 2019.

21. Klein, Gary. "Performing a project premortem." *Harvard Business Review* 85, no. 9 (2007): 18–19. (Careful readers will note that I wrote about pre-mortems in Pink, Daniel H. *When: The scientific secrets of perfect timing.* New York: Riverhead, 2019, 107–108.)

22. Stillman, Jessica. "How Amazon's Jeff Bezos made one of the toughest decisions of his career." *Inc.*, June 13, 2016.

23. Wilson, Timothy D., and Daniel T. Gilbert. "Affective forecasting: Knowing what to want." *Current Directions in Psychological Science* 14, no. 3 (2005): 131–34; Gilbert, Daniel T., Matthew D. Lieberman, Carey K. Morewedge, and Timothy D. Wilson. "The peculiar longevity of things not so bad." *Psychological Science* 15, no. 1 (2004): 14–19. See also Crawford, Matthew T., Allen R. McConnell, Amy C. Lewis, and Steven J. Sherman. "Reactance, compliance, and anticipated regret." *Journal of Experimental Social Psychology* 38, no. 1 (2002): 56–63.

24. Gilbert, Daniel T., Carey K. Morewedge, Jane L. Risen, and Timothy D. Wilson. "Looking forward to looking backward: The misprediction of regret." *Psychological Science* 15, no. 5 (2004): 346–50. See also Sevdalis, Nick, and Nigel Harvey. "Biased forecasting of postdecisional affect." *Psychological Science* 18, no. 8 (2007): 678–81.

25. Simonson, Itamar. "The influence of anticipating regret and responsibility on purchase decisions." *Journal of Consumer Research* 19, no. 1 (1992): 105–118.

26. Bar-Hillel, Maya, and Efrat Neter. "Why are people reluctant to exchange lottery tickets?" *Journal of Personality and Social Psychology* 70, no. 1 (1996): 17; Risen, Jane L., and Thomas Gilovich. "Another look at why people are reluctant to exchange lottery tickets." *Journal of Personality and Social Psychology* 93, no. 1 (2007): 12. (People also believe that exchanging their lottery ticket increases the likelihood that it will win.)

27. van de Ven, Niels, and Marcel Zeelenberg. "Regret aversion and the reluctance to exchange lottery tickets." *Journal of Economic Psychology* 32, no. 1 (2011): 194–200.

28. Beattie, Jane, Jonathan Baron, John C. Hershey, and Mark D. Spranca. "Psychological determinants of decision attitude." *Journal of Behavioral Decision Making* 7, no. 2 (1994): 129–44; Wake, Sean, Jolie Wormwood, and Ajay B. Satpute. "The influence of fear on risk taking: A meta-analysis." *Cognition and Emotion* 34, no. 6 (2020): 1143–59; McConnell, Allen R., Keith E. Niedermeier, Jill M. Leibold, Amani G. El-Alayli, Peggy P. Chin, and Nicole M. Kuiper. "What if I find it cheaper someplace else? Role of prefactual thinking and anticipated regret in consumer behavior." *Psychology and Marketing* 17, no. 4 (2000): 281–98. (Price guarantees can overcome the inertia of consumers not buying because they fear prices will drop.)

29. Larrick, Richard P., and Terry L. Boles. "Avoiding regret in decisions with feedback: A negotiation example." *Organizational Behavior and Human Decision Processes* 63, no. 1 (1995): 87–97.

Notes

30. Merry, Justin W., Mary Kate Elenchin, and Renee N. Surma. "Should students change their answers on multiple choice questions?" *Advances in Physiology Education* 45, no. 1 (2021): 182–90; Princeton Review. "Fourteen avoidable mistakes you make on test day." Available at: https://www.princetonreview.com/college-advice/test-day-mistakes.

31. Merry, Justin W., Mary Kate Elenchin, and Renee N. Surma. "Should students change their answers on multiple choice questions?" *Advances in Physiology Education* 45, no. 1 (2021): 182–90; Bauer, Daniel, Veronika Kopp, and Martin R. Fischer. "Answer changing in multiple choice assessment: Change that answer when in doubt—and spread the word!" *BMC Medical Education* 7, no. 1 (2007): 1–5; Couchman, Justin J., Noelle E. Miller, Shaun J. Zmuda, Kathryn Feather, and Tina Schwartzmeyer. "The instinct fallacy: The metacognition of answering and revising during college exams." *Metacognition and Learning* 11, no. 2 (2016): 171–85. (What matters is less first instincts or not, but metacognition—how confident students are in their answers.)

32. Kruger, Justin, Derrick Wirtz, and Dale T. Miller. "Counterfactual thinking and the first instinct fallacy." *Journal of Personality and Social Psychology* 88, no. 5 (2005): 725.

33. Simon, Herbert A. "Rational choice and the structure of the environment." *Psychological Review* 63, no. 2 (1956): 129; Simon, Herbert A. "Rational decision making in business organizations." *American Economic Review* 69, no. 4 (1979): 493–513.

34. Schwartz, Barry, Andrew Ward, John Monterosso, Sonja Lyubomirsky, Katherine White, and Darrin R. Lehman. "Maximizing versus satisficing: Happiness is a matter of choice." *Journal of Personality and Social Psychology* 83, no. 5 (2002): 1178.

35. Schwartz, Barry, Andrew Ward, John Monterosso, Sonja Lyubomirsky, Katherine White, and Darrin R. Lehman. "Maximizing versus satisficing: Happiness is a matter of choice." *Journal of Personality and Social Psychology* 83, no. 5 (2002): 1178. ("The more options there are, the more likely one is to make a suboptimal choice and this prospect may undermine whatever pleasure one gets from the actual choice.")

Coda: Regret and Redemption

1. McAdams, Dan P., and P. J. Bowman. "Narrating life's turning points: Redemption and contamination: Narrative studies of lives in transition." In *Turns in the road: Narrative studies of lives in transition.* Washington, DC: American Psychological Association Press, 2001; McAdams, Dan P., Jeffrey Reynolds, Martha Lewis, Allison H. Patten, and Phillip J. Bowman. "When bad things turn good and good things turn bad: Sequences of redemption and contamination in life narrative and their relation to psychosocial adaptation in midlife adults and in students." *Personality and Social Psychology Bulletin* 27, no. 4 (2001): 474–85; McAdams, Dan P. "The psychology of life stories." *Review of General Psychology* 5, no. 2 (2001): 100–122; McAdams, Dan P. *The redemptive self: Stories Americans live by*, revised and expanded edition. New York: Oxford University Press, 2013.

Index

Index

Index

Index

Index

Index

Index

Index

Index

Index